HOW TO THINK LIKE

SIGMUND
FREUD

HOW TO THINK LIKE

SIGMUND FREUD

DANIEL SMITH

Michael O'Mara Books Limited

For Rosie and Lottie and Matt

First published in Great Britain in 2017 by
Michael O'Mara Books Limited
9 Lion Yard
Tremadoc Road
London SW4 7NQ

A CIP catalogue record for this book is available from the British Library.

Papers used by Michael O'Mara Books Limited are natural, recyclable
products made from wood grown in sustainable forests. The manufacturing
processes conform to the environmental regulations of the country of origin.

ISBN: 978-1-78243-702-4 in hardback print format
ISBN: 978-1-78243-706-2 in paperback print format
ISBN: 978-1-78243-704-8 in ebook format

1 3 5 7 9 10 8 6 4 2

Designed and typeset by Envy Design Ltd

Printed and bound by CPI Group (UK) Ltd, Croydon, CR0 4YY

www.mombooks.com

Contents

Introduction

'Sigmund Freud was a novelist with a scientific background. He just didn't know he was a novelist. All those damn psychiatrists after him, they didn't know he was a novelist either.'

JOHN IRVING IN *WRITERS AT WORK: THE PARIS REVIEW INTERVIEWS*, 1988

Of all the subjects in the How to Think Like series, Sigmund Freud is perhaps the most enigmatic. As the father of psychoanalysis, he introduced the world to the scientific conception of the unconscious and compelled us to explore the dark recesses of the human psyche – notably through analysis of our dreams and our streams of thought. He was also responsible for a sea change in attitudes to mental illness. Where people had once been cast out as variously physiologically compromised, morally degenerate or even agents of devilry, Freud offered hope that the causes of psychological imbalance could be discovered and addressed.

He was, too, a quite brilliant iconoclast, overturning received wisdom and questioning orthodoxies. A born outsider, he was fearless in challenging social elites and intellectual complacency. Furthermore, his ideas permeated the wider culture. They are evident in our films, TV, music and literature. They are taught in classrooms and lecture theatres. They have been absorbed into our very language. It is thanks to Freud that we season our everyday conversation with terms such as the unconscious, the ego, the libido, the Oedipus complex, penis envy, the Freudian slip, the psychiatrist's couch, anally retentive … the list goes on. Indeed, he is one of those few individuals whose name gains adjectival status.

It is no overstatement to say he originated concepts that allow us to view the world differently. He redirected our gaze from the world around us and its constructions – the universe, society, theology – to the world within us – our psyches. It is worth noting that the window above Freud's desk was adorned with a mirror that permanently enabled him to look at himself even while he stared out on the world. Psychologist and Freud academic John Kihlstrom has said, 'More than Einstein or Watson and Crick, more than Hitler or Lenin, Roosevelt or Kennedy, more than Picasso, Eliot, or Stravinsky, more than the Beatles or Bob Dylan, Freud's influence on modern culture has been profound and long-lasting.'

Yet, his legacy remains a mixed one. Scientific progress has unquestionably overtaken him since his death in 1939. That which he had a tendency to frame as scientific truth has often been shown up as speculation, opinion or conjecture. Such fundamental tenets as the id, ego and superego, his model of psychosexual development, and his theories of dream interpretation have been largely discredited. As Albert Einstein noted of him: 'He had a sharp vision; no illusions lulled him to sleep except for an often exaggerated faith in his own ideas.' So Freud's theories are rarely used directly in clinical practice today. Yet his role in the scientific exploration of the mind should not be dismissed. While much of his work has been shown as incomplete and sometimes wrong, he brought a new energy to the scientific study of the psyche that paved the way for the developments that now benefit us. In the words of his recent biographer, Adam Phillips, Freud 'shows us how ingenious we are in not knowing ourselves'.

It is advisable, then, to position Freud not as a scientist in the current sense but as a cultural icon. The celebrated literary critic Harold Bloom said in 2006:

> Sigmund Freud persists today, but not as a scientist or even as a healer. The late Francis Crick observed that Freud was a Viennese physician who wrote a very good prose style, but while funny enough, that is hardly adequate. Freud matters because he shares in the qualities of Proust and Joyce: cognitive insight, stylistic splendour, wisdom.

His personal life, meanwhile, was complex and intriguing. He was a figure of many internal contradictions – an atheist greatly influenced by his Jewishness, a firm friend until he became a fierce enemy, a man who hungered for wealth and fame but resented the constraints they imposed. His marriage lasted into five decades, yet there is evidence that he strayed from the marital bed

Introduction

(though probably while keeping things 'in the family'). His professional life, on the other hand, forced him to look deep into himself. Writing in 1905, he said, 'No one who, like me, conjures up the most evil of those half-tamed demons that inhabit the human beast, and seeks to wrestle with them, can expect to come through the struggle unscathed.' The nature of his work demanded that he reveal something of himself to the world at large – he was the subject of numerous of his own papers – yet he famously decried the art of biography and fiercely guarded his privacy. Getting to the 'real' Freud is thus a testing – though always invigorating – challenge.

This book necessarily explores many of the groundbreaking 'big ideas' that Freud introduced over his lifetime. However, it does not aim to serve as a replacement for reading his works in their original form. Most of them, anyway, are eminently readable – he was awarded the 1930 Goethe prize for literature for his 'clear and impeccable style', an accolade that infuriated him for its recognition of the quality of his writing and not his scientific insight. This volume aims merely to explore Freud the man – his personality, inspirations, motivations, ideas and methods.

Let me begin by quoting from a passage that Freud wrote in 1932 for an introduction to a book offering a psychological study of the former US president, Woodrow Wilson. He might have been writing about himself:

Fools, visionaries, sufferers from delusions, neurotics and lunatics have played great roles at all times in the history of mankind, and not merely when the accident of birth had bequeathed them sovereignty. Usually they have wreaked havoc; but not always. Such persons have exercised far-reaching influence upon their own and later times, they have given impetus to important cultural movements and have made great discoveries. They have been able to accomplish such achievements on the one hand through the help of the intact portion of their personalities, that is to say in spite of their abnormalities; but on the other hand it is often precisely the pathological traits of their characters, the one-sidedness of their development, the abnormal strengthening of certain desires, the uncritical and unrestrained abandonment to a single aim, which give them the power to drag others after them and to overcome the resistance of the world.

Landmarks in a Remarkable Life

1856   Sigismund Freud is born on 6 May 1856 in Freiberg, Moravia, in the Austrian Empire.

1860   The Freuds move to Vienna after a brief spell in Leipzig.

1865   Sigmund begins to attend the Leopoldstadter Communal Gymnasium school.

1873   Freud is persuaded to study medicine at the University of Vienna after hearing Goethe's essay 'On Nature'.

1876   He begins working in the laboratory of Ernst Brücke.

1881   Freud graduates as a doctor of medicine after a long eight years.

1882   Martha Bernays agrees to marry Freud.

1883   He takes a post in Theodor Meynert's psychiatric clinic.

1884	He begins research into the medicinal effects of cocaine.
1885	Jean-Martin Charcot mentors Freud at the Salpêtrière Hospital in Paris, introducing him to hypnosis.
1886	Freud sets himself up in private practice and marries Martha Bernays.
1887	A daughter, Mathilda, is born. Freud also forms a friendship with Wilhelm Fliess.
1889	A son, Jean-Martin, is born.
1891	Freud's *On Aphasia* is his first published work. Another son, Oliver, is born.
1892	A third son, Ernst, is born.
1893	A daughter, Sophie, is born.
1895	Freud and Josef Breuer publish *Studies on Hysteria*. Another daughter, Anna, is born.
1896	Freud's father, Jacob, dies. Freud uses the term 'psychoanalysis' for the first time.
1897	He undertakes a three-year-long self-analysis.
1899	*The Interpretation of Dreams* is published.
1900	Treatment of 'Dora' begins.
1902	The Wednesday Psychological Society is founded at Freud's home in Vienna.
1904	Freud begins a correspondence with Eugen Bleuler.
1905	Publication of *Jokes and Their Relation to the Unconscious*, *Three Essays on the Theory of*

the 'death drive', is published. Freud's daughter Sophie dies.

1921   Publishes *Group Psychology and the Analysis of the Ego*.

1923   Freud is diagnosed with cancer of the jaw and palate. His grandson Heinz dies. *The Ego and the Id* is published.

1925   Publication of *An Autobiographical Study*.

1927   Publication of *The Future of an Illusion*.

1930   Freud publishes *Civilization and its Discontents*. His mother, Amalia, dies.

1933   Publication of *New Introductory Lectures on Psychoanalysis* and *Why War?*, a correspondence between Freud and Albert Einstein. Freud's works are publicly burned in Nazi Germany.

1938   Germany annexes Austria. Freud's house and the headquarters of the Vienna Association of Psychoanalysis are raided and Anna Freud is arrested by the Gestapo. Freud and his family emigrate to London.

1939   Freud dies on 23 September. *Moses and Monotheism* is published.

1940   Publication of the unfinished *An Outline of Psychoanalysis*.

1951   The death of Martha Freud.

Plan Early
for Greatness

'A man who has been the indisputable favourite of his
mother keeps for life the feeling of a conqueror, that
confidence of success that often induces real success.'

SIGMUND FREUD, 1917

1

Sigismund Schlomo Freud was born on 6 May 1856 in the city of Freiberg, Moravia, in what was then part of Austria-Hungary (Freiberg is now called Příbor and lies within the Czech Republic). He was the first child of the marriage of Jacob Freud, a moderately successful wool merchant, and Amalia Nathansohn. Jacob was considerably older than his wife, having been previously married. Already a father of two, he would go on to have six further children with Amalia.

A year after Sigi (as the family called him) was born, a brother (named Julius) came along. Julius invoked feelings of jealousy and resentment in his older brother and Julius' death in 1858 would cause Sigi lingering feelings of guilt in years to come. Nonetheless, Freud came to regard his early years in Freiberg as, overall, a period of tranquillity and happiness. Writing in 1931, he said of Freiberg, 'Of one thing I am certain: deep within me, although overlaid, there continues to live the happy child from Freiberg, the first-born son of a youthful mother, the boy who received from this air, from this soil, the first indelible impressions.'

However, this time in paradise was to be short-lived. With Jacob's business faltering, the family moved to Leipzig in 1859 and to Vienna the following year, when Sigi was four years old. Vienna was one of the great capitals of Europe and then at the peak of its power, yet Freud found it dismal and unwelcoming. In particular, he came to resent the undercurrent of anti-Semitism that was building a head of steam at the time. Although his parents were largely non-observant, Freud experienced for the first time the animosity of strangers towards his Jewish heritage. As we shall see, it would have a huge impact on the rest of his life, both professionally and personally.

His feelings towards Vienna were also coloured by the fact that the Freuds spent a large period of their stay living in stifling poverty. Yet for all that, the young Sigi enjoyed a standard of life superior to that of his siblings, on account of his being the favourite of his mother. She took to calling him 'My golden Sigi', and he enjoyed the best of the little that there was. By 1866, for example, when there were two adults and seven children to accommodate, Sigi was the only one to have his own room, and where the other children had to make do with candles, he was allowed a gas lamp.

This was in part because he was already emerging as an extraordinary scholar. After initially being schooled at home, he entered the Leopoldstadter Communal Gymnasium (a German grammar school) and sat at the top of his class for each of the seven years that he was there. He was also wily in his choice of schoolmates, generally gravitating to those fellow pupils who could assist him in his studies. Among them was Heinrich Braun, who in due course would make his own mark on the world as a prominent Social Democratic politician. Freud, Braun, another boy Eduard Silberstein, and three brothers by the name of Fluss formed the *Bund*, a discussion group that regularly met at a local café to ponder important questions of life, the universe and everything. The Flusses also contributed to Freud's education by introducing him to their sister and mother, both of whom Freud felt a great attachment to. They no doubt played an unwitting role in his development of the comprehensive theory of sexuality that he would evolve later in his career.

Amalia, meanwhile, did all she could to make life as easy as possible for her golden boy. Freud's younger sister, Anna, would recall how the piano on which she was learning to play was removed from the family home because her big brother had complained that the noise was too disturbing. The relationship between Amalia and Freud would remain extraordinarily close for the remainder of her life. Freud made the statement at the beginning of this chapter in reference to Johann Wolfgang von Goethe, that great German man of letters from an earlier generation, but it just as accurately describes him. In the *New Introductory Lectures* of 1933, he would say that 'a mother is only brought unlimited satisfaction by her relation to a son: that is altogether the most perfect, the most free from ambivalence of all human relationships.'

Despite his unpromising start in Vienna – a city that over the years inveigled itself into his affection so that towards the end of his life he would describe it as a 'prison' but one 'I still loved greatly' – Freud arrived at the cusp of adulthood full of ambition to do great things. Naturally talented academically, his confidence that he would achieve notable feats was fuelled by the unequivocal support and adoration of his mother, who had set up her family so as to allow Golden Sigi the best chance to prosper. As he would recall many years later, by the time he was eighteen he had a 'premonition of a task ahead' that 'I might, during the course of my life, contribute something to our human knowledge'.

POWER TO THE OUTSIDER

'… as a Jew I was prepared to join the Opposition and to do without agreement with the compact majority.'

SIGMUND FREUD, 1926

Where some individuals achieve greatness by tapping into the mainstream of thought, Freud was one of those who owed his reputation to challenging orthodoxy. His greatness, it might be said, came as a result of persuading the world to accept his own heterodox theses as orthodox.

His sense of being an outsider started early among the social circles he inhabited in Vienna, and it had two chief causes. The first of these was economic. As we have seen, the Freuds faced an almost permanent financial struggle during his childhood, largely inhabiting the poorer districts of a city that boasted hugely affluent neighbourhoods – especially given Vienna's position as the jewel in the crown of the Austro-Hungarian Empire. While Freud lived cheek-by-jowl with the powerful and well-to-do, he could only look in on this world rather than participate in it. Although this was not a comfortable position to be in, it did allow him the freedom to critique the world as he saw it.

The second cause was his Jewish background. Anti-Semitism was on the rise in Europe in the latter half of the nineteenth century and was rife in Vienna while Freud lived there. Indeed, it is likely that Freud adapted his name from Sigismund to Sigmund while in his early twenties in part because Sigismund was a standard name used in generic 'Jew jokes'. Furthermore, one of the defining moments of his childhood came when he was aged twelve and his father related the details of an anti-Semitic attack he had suffered many years earlier. Jacob had been living in Galicia in Poland at the time, prior to his move to Freiberg. He was walking along the street one day when a Christian man approached him and knocked off his hat. He then shouted at him: 'Jew! Get off the pavement!' Freud asked his father how he responded to such an outrage. Jacob replied that he did nothing other than to step into the road to retrieve his hat.

This revelation left Freud with a mixture of emotions. On the one hand, he felt profound disappointment that his father had failed to stick up for himself. On the other, it fuelled his burning sense of injustice that anyone might deem it acceptable to treat another person in this way simply because they were of Jewish origin. But it also left him with the overwhelming conviction that in order to succeed in life, he must do it on his own terms. He would not seek the approval of others in his quest to extend human knowledge, nor would he confine himself to imposed modes of thinking. Finding himself excluded from the full spectrum of social opportunity, he discerned a chance to challenge the complacent assumptions of society. As he would write in 1926:

… to my Jewish nature alone … I owed two characteristics that had become indispensable to me in the difficult course of my life. Because I was a Jew I found myself free from many prejudices which restricted others in the use of their intellect; and as a Jew I was prepared to join the Opposition and to do without agreement with the compact majority.

Freud could hardly be said to have enjoyed his outsider status. His family's poverty birthed in him a desire to earn enough throughout the rest of his life to allay financial worries, and anti-Semitism never failed to enrage him. We also get a sense of his frustration at non-acceptance in his response to a lecture he gave at the Viennese Psychiatric Society early on in his career. Writing in 1896 to his great friend of the time, Wilhelm Fliess, he said the talk 'was given an icy reception by the asses and a strange evaluation by Krafft-Ebing [Richard von Krafft-Ebing, a fellow Austro-Hungarian psychiatrist]: "It sounds like a scientific fairy tale." And this, after one has demonstrated to them the solution of a millennia-old problem … They can go to hell, euphemistically expressed.'

Yet he also recognized that being on the outside looking in was a crucial component of his identity and allowed him to follow intellectual paths down which others feared to venture. The confidence he took from his mother's unstinting acceptance and promotion of his interests ensured he never buckled under the pressure of non-acceptance by others. Instead, he used his outsider status to daringly critique the accepted ideas of his time and to experiment with truly *outré* modes of thinking.

Freud's Heroes

'Hannibal, whom I had come to resemble
in these respects, had been the favourite
hero of my later schooldays.'

SIGMUND FREUD, *THE INTERPRETATION
OF DREAMS*, 1900

Over the course of his life, there was a plethora of figures for whom Freud proclaimed admiration – among them physicians and scientists (many of whom he worked with), and writers, artists and philosophers. However, this roll call of genuine heroes – those towering figures of humanity, as opposed to mere giants in a particular field of expertise – was significantly smaller.

His two great heroes of science were Nicolaus Copernicus and Charles Darwin. Some three centuries earlier, Copernicus had caused an intellectual revolution by positing that the sun and not the Earth was at the centre of the universe. Darwin's theory of evolution, meanwhile, gained broad acceptance during Freud's youth (as Freud noted, his theories 'held out hopes of an extraordinary advance in our understanding of the world'). Their importance to him was not merely in the unquestionable quality of their scientific work but also because they qualitatively changed our concept of the entire world and our place within it. They had been the prime instigators of what he regarded as the two great shocks to man's complacency – an achievement that greatly appealed to him. In *A General Introduction to Psychoanalysis*, published in 1920, he would say of these shocks (or 'outrages', as he called them):

The first was when it realized that our earth was not the centre of the universe, but only a tiny speck in a world-system of a magnitude hardly conceivable; this is associated in our minds with the name of Copernicus, although Alexandrian doctrines taught something very similar. The second was when biological research robbed man of his peculiar privilege of having been specially created, and relegated him to a descent from the animal world, implying an ineradicable animal nature in him: this transvaluation has been accomplished in our own time upon the instigation of Charles Darwin, Wallace [British naturalist Alfred Wallace], and their predecessors, and not without the most violent opposition from their contemporaries.

But to bring about a similar 'outrage' was ultimately Freud's aspiration too, and one he felt he had significantly achieved by persuading considerable swathes of the world in his own lifetime that the solutions to many of the mysteries of humanity are not to be found by looking outwards but instead by turning our gaze inwards. We might well think that Freud may also have elevated Albert Einstein to his pantheon of scientific heroes, for his general theory of relativity brought about a similar recalibration of human thought. Freud certainly admired him and engaged in an important correspondence with him in the 1930s, although the fact that Einstein's magnum opus did not appear until Freud was already in his sixties mitigated against his induction into the revered group.

Away from science, he cited a couple of historical figures that at first glance may appear somewhat eccentric choices. One was Oliver Cromwell, the Puritan military and political leader in the English Civil War in the seventeenth century, who signed the death warrant of King Charles I and himself became the dictatorial Lord Protector of the realm. How did such a figure come to capture the imagination of the youthful Freud, rather than, say, any of the great historical figures of his native central Europe? He even chose to name one of his sons Oliver in honour of Cromwell.

The answer may partially lie in an 1882 letter in which Freud reflected on his first trip to Britain. He spoke warmly of the country's 'sober industrious ... and sensitive feeling for justice' – features which it may be argued were socially ingrained by the Civil War and personally reflected in Cromwell's character. Furthermore, Cromwell had ordered one particular action that chimed with Freud as a victim of prejudice against Jews – he had permitted Jews to reside once more in Britain after they had been expelled some four hundred years earlier. It is intriguing to ponder whether Freud might also have been drawn to Cromwell because of his participation in the regicide – an act with parallels to the Oedipal Complex that Freud so famously described.

But another figure stood head and shoulders above even Cromwell in Freud's estimation – Hannibal, the great leader of Carthage in North Africa, who defeated the might of the Roman Empire in the Second Punic War (218–01 BC). Freud expanded upon the quotation at the beginning of this section to explain what drew him to Hannibal:

Like so many boys of that age, I had sympathized in the Punic Wars not with the Romans but with the Carthaginians. And when in the higher classes I began to understand for the first time what it meant to belong to an alien race, and anti-Semitic feelings among the other boys warned me that I must take up a definite position, the figure of the Semitic general rose still higher in my esteem ...To my youthful mind Hannibal and Rome symbolized the conflict between the tenacity of Jewry and the organization of the Catholic Church.

Hannibal was one of the great outsider figures of history, the underdog who took on 'the Establishment' (in the shape of Rome) and won against all the odds. It was a model of existence that had natural appeal for Freud, who upset the established intellectual order every bit as effectively as Hannibal managed to militarily. In addition, Hannibal specifically represented the Semite while Rome stood for the Roman Catholic Church (although, of course, Hannibal was dealing with a pre-Christian Rome), that force Freud deemed in large part responsible for the anti-Semitic climate that he was forced to endure on a daily basis.

Hannibal seems to have taken on particular significance for Freud after he learned of the anti-Semitic attack against his father in Galicia. While Freud wrestled with Jacob's apparent capitulation, he no doubt was drawn to Hannibal's reported oath that he would avenge himself on all Romans.

Discern Your True Field of Interest

'A man like me cannot live without a
hobby-horse, a consuming passion …'

FREUD TO WILHELM FLIESS, 1895

Such was the range of Freud's intellect that by the time he went to university (at the unusually early age of seventeen), it was by no means certain in which academic direction he would go. His old friend, Heinrich Braun, suggested he should become a lawyer but Freud felt a more natural affinity to the sciences. The question was eventually decided when he attended a public lecture at which an essay on nature Freud attributed to Goethe (but which was possibly actually written by Georg Christoph Tobler) was read aloud. Freud described it as 'beautiful' and concluded that he should study medicine.

He enrolled at the University of Vienna in 1873 but the experience was far from satisfying. Apart from enduring yet more anti-Semitism, he also quickly realized he was less drawn to medicine in all its nitty-gritty detail than to the pursuit of broader scientific truths. Despite a plea to his sister Anna that 'I want to help people who suffer,' his focus quickly drifted from the syllabus of his degree to more esoteric scientific research projects. As a result, it would be fully eight years before he was awarded his medical degree. In 1876, for instance, he was awarded a research grant that allowed him to travel to Trieste. There he worked alongside prominent Darwinist Carl Claus at a zoological research station, dissecting hundreds of eels in order to study their sexual organs. If it had been a dream, Freud might have made much of its rich symbolism later on in his career.

In 1877, and by then back in Vienna, he took a position in the research laboratory of Ernst Brücke. Brücke was one of the leading lights of mechanism – a school of thought that believes all phenomena of life result from the same physical and chemical laws that govern inorganic matter. He would have a lasting influence on Freud, both in terms of ideas and career development. Under his guidance, Freud became an expert in histology (concerned with organic tissue) and neurophysiology (relating to the nervous system). In particular, he carried out work to determine the similarities and differences between human and frog nerve cells, reaching the conclusion that the nervous systems of higher and lower lifeforms are constructed of the same basic material. In other words, a man is not a frog not because he is made of something fundamentally different but only because of the elevated level of complication in his physiology.

Freud stayed with Brücke until 1882, a year after his graduation from university, which proved something of a crunch year. Freud had recently met and fallen in love with the sister of a friend, Martha Bernays. The two were quickly engaged and Freud turned his mind to how he might be able to support a wife and family. Brücke laid out his options in stark terms: medical research was not well paid at the best of times, there was little possibility of advancement in his own lab, and Freud's chances of promotion elsewhere were severely limited by the currents of anti-Semitism swirling around.

Freud decided his best hope was to embrace medical practice in a manner he had hitherto failed to do. He took a job at Vienna's general hospital with a view to building up his practical experience before launching into the more profitable field of private practice. However, he still struggled to enjoy clinical medicine, and even under the tutelage of the highly respected Hermann Nothnagel the discipline of surgery was, for Freud, deeply boring.

However, he found his next move – to the psychiatry department of Theodor Meynert in 1883 – far more rewarding. Taken under Meynert's wing, Freud discovered he was deeply interested in neuropathology – complaints of the nervous system – while Meynert's conviction that some forms of neuroses were reversible would inform his illustrious pupil's later work. Freud was now beginning to find his professional feet and it exhilarated him, as his letters to Martha in this period show. 'I am very stubborn and very reckless and need great challenges,' he told her in 1884. 'I have done a number of things which any sensible person would be bound to consider very rash ... my way of life: risking a lot, hoping a lot, working a lot. To average bourgeois common sense I have been lost long ago.'

In the same year he worked on an innovative technique of staining brain tissue for examination under the microscope – a development that won him much respect among his peers even as perfection of the process proved elusive. To Martha he wrote, 'As you know, an explorer's temperament requires two basic qualities: optimism in attempt, criticism in work.' The next major step along his career path came in 1885, when he was invited to Paris to study at the Salpêtrière Hospital under the noted neurologist, Jean-Martin Charcot.

TAKE THE PATH LESS TRAVELLED

'My tyrant is psychology.'
SIGMUND FREUD TO WILHELM FLIESS, 1895

Charcot was, among other things, the first clinician to describe multiple sclerosis and the chance to study with him filled Freud with unadulterated excitement, which he shared with Martha:

Oh, how wonderful it will be! I am coming with money and staying a long time and bringing something beautiful for you and then go on to Paris and become a great scholar and then come back to Vienna with a huge, enormous halo, and then we will soon get married, and I will cure all the incurable nervous cases

and through you I shall be healthy and I will go on
kissing you till you are strong and gay and happy ...

Charcot's work drove Freud towards a renewed
evaluation of how the mind can precipitate the physical
symptoms within a patient. He also pushed Freud away
from his recent research into brain anatomy towards the
study of neuroses. In particular, Charcot was fostering
some revolutionary ideas concerning hysteria – a term
now rarely used in a medical sense but which at the time
referred to a disorder characterized by the conversion
of stress (caused by an initial traumatic event) into
physical symptoms. These might include fits, paralysis,
sleepwalking, hallucination, and loss of speech, memory
and sensation. It was traditionally considered either to
be an imagined condition or else caused by irritation
of the female genitalia. Charcot, however, disagreed. It
was not imaginary, he insisted, nor was it a uniquely
female condition. Furthermore, he argued that it was
not the result of an anatomical cause at all but came
about because of a malfunction in analytical processes.
In other words, hysteria was an emotional response to
a physical index accident (for instance, the emotional
processing of being in a coaching accident). Charcot's
ideas sowed the seeds that Freud would cultivate into
his belief that any traumatic event (even if not resulting
in physical harm) could lead to unconscious symptom-
formation. Despite his own concerns about its effects,

Charcot subjected patients to hypnosis as a means to identify the condition.

When his five-month internship came to an end, Freud returned to Vienna set upon a path away from neurology and towards psychiatry. He had even offered to translate Charcot's lectures into German so that he might win the ongoing goodwill of his new mentor while also making a name for them both among the German-speaking medical establishment. However, Freud's reabsorption into the Viennese scene was far from triumphant. The new theories he proffered concerning hysteria and hypnotism received a sceptical – if not downright hostile – reception, especially given that Charcot had the ill-grace to not only not be Austrian but to be French to boot. It was a talk Freud gave on hysteria that brought about the criticisms that prompted his condemnation of the 'asses' at the Viennese Psychiatric Society.

Nonetheless, Freud had at last found his true professional passion – psychiatry and the mysteries of the human mind. It would be several years before he could devote his energies exclusively to the discipline – only in 1896 did he tell Fliess: 'As a young man I knew no longing other than for philosophical knowledge, and now I am about to fulfil it as I move from medicine to psychology.' But he was now on the path that would deliver him fame and notoriety. As he put it in 1895, again to Fliess: 'I have found my tyrant, and in his service I know no limits. My tyrant is psychology.'

Make a Name
for Yourself

'I have often felt as though I had inherited all the
defiance and all the passions with which our ancestors
defended their Temple and could gladly sacrifice
my life for one great moment in history.'

SIGMUND FREUD TO MARTHA BERNAYS, 1886

Freud owed his professional success to a number of factors, not least his expansive and fearlessly investigative intellect. However, the role of his personal ambition should not be underestimated. So what lay behind his drive, beyond a pure desire to extend humanity's understanding of ourselves and our world? What led him to knock at doors behind which lay who knew what potential monsters? In part, at least, it was the poverty that blighted his childhood.

Jacob Freud's fortunes had taken an all but fatal hit in 1873 when his business collapsed. As the great hope of the family, the burden to become the main support to his parents and siblings no doubt weighed heavily on the young Freud's shoulders. After he met Martha Bernays, that pressure only increased, and once again when the couple married in 1886 and planned to build a family (they had three boys and three girls between 1887 and 1895). Having been told by Brücke that his career prospects were restricted through no fault of his own, but simply because of his Jewish background,

Freud was prepared to make bold moves to push himself up the career ladder. Left in no doubt that merit alone was insufficient, he seemed to accept that he may have no choice but to make enemies as he sought to promote his work. Hence his willingness to deliver his lecture on hysteria in what he must have known would be a hostile environment.

Furthermore, the anti-Jewish sentiment he had endured since early childhood caused him to grow a thick skin. Indeed, while specific criticisms may have rankled, he appears to have on some level enjoyed the rough-and-tumble of academic life. As we shall see in later chapters, he routinely cultivated friendships to the point that they promoted his professional interests, but was ruthless in cutting people off if he considered they posed a threat to his professional standing.

Freud also had a knack for brilliantly marketing ideas that in other hands might have been at best opaque or at worst alienating to the world at large. Of course, it took time for Freud's theories to wend their way into mainstream discourse (his early works initially sold in dribbles rather than torrents), but over his lifetime he sold psychoanalysis to the world. Without his dynamism and storytelling flair, the whole movement would likely have become little more than a footnote in the medical textbooks. Just consider how Freud's language has been adopted into mainstream discourse. In 1896, he was the originator of the very term *psychoanalysis*, and without him we would not now talk freely of the Oedipus complex, narcissism, the ego and id, the libido, death wishes or even anal retentiveness. If he had not been a genius of psychiatry, he could surely have had a stellar career as an advertising executive.

Like others of history's great achievers, Freud had that potent combination of talent, ambition and the ability to communicate to a wide audience.

Recognize a
Dead End

'A little cocaine, to untie my tongue.'

SIGMUND FREUD TO MARTHA BERNAYS, 1886

While Freud's career was distinguished by his commitment to an array of innovative and controversial ideas in the face of often intense opposition, he also had the good sense to recognize and abandon certain errors he made upon the way.

One of the most striking instances of this dates to the 1880s, a decade in which Freud took a close interest in the possible medical advantages of cocaine. This was an age, it should be remembered, in which the dangers of cocaine as we understand them today were entirely unknown. Indeed, these were the days when the coca leaf, from which cocaine is derived, was about to be used as an active ingredient in the soon-to-be invented Coca-Cola. Freud's own interest in the drug seems to have been piqued after he heard that it was used to revive ailing soldiers while out on manoeuvres. As he put it many years later: 'In 1884, a side but deep interest made me have the Merck company supply me with an alkaloid quite little known at the time, to study its physiological effects.'

He began to self-medicate and was initially in thrall to its quasi-magical effects. Before long, he had introduced

Martha to it as well. Later that year he published an article ('On Coca') in a Viennese magazine, which was, to all intents and purposes, a hymn of praise to the wonder drug. He even promised that additional uses for cocaine would soon come to light. So it came to pass when Freud bumped into an old friend who told him he was suffering from severe intestinal pain. Freud prescribed him a 5 per cent cocaine solution, which led to the patient reporting numbness on his tongue and lips after taking it. Freud now pondered the possible anaesthetic properties of the drug. He suggested to a doctor friend who specialized in treating eyes to investigate whether it might serve to anaesthetize patients undergoing ophthalmic operations.

Shortly afterwards, Freud went on a trip to visit Martha. On his return, he discovered that another friend, Carl Koller, had addressed an ophthalmology congress in Heidelberg to announce cocaine's properties as an anaesthetic. Freud thus missed out on the recognition he believed he was due. However, it was not long before he began desperately back-pedalling in his support of the drug. His change of heart was the result of his involvement in the tragic demise of a friend, the physiologist Ernst von Fleischl-Marxow.

Sometime earlier, von Fleischl-Marxow had started taking morphine to relieve the pain caused by an infection. By 1885 he was firmly addicted, so Freud suggested a switch to cocaine to wean him off morphine. However, the physiologist merely replaced one horrible addiction with another and started to use cocaine in copious volumes.

Six years of abuse, coupled with chronic pain and other symptoms, culminated in his death in 1891. It was not long after he had pushed his friend towards the drug that Freud realized it was both highly addictive and dangerous. He put his professional dalliance with cocaine to bed (though it is possible he used it himself into the 1890s) and effectively wrote the misbegotten episode out of his curriculum vitae. The guilt associated with von Fleischl-Marxow's decline was, though, more difficult to shrug off.

Indeed, it was likely one of the reasons why Freud burned all of his personal and academic papers in 1885 – an event to the chagrin of his many biographers. It seems to have been at once an effort to liberate himself from the memory of the errors he had made in his juvenile years, and a bid to ensure that the rest of the world should never get wind of them. As he put it to Martha: '… all my thoughts and feelings about the world in general and about myself in particular have been found unworthy of further existence.' Interestingly, it was a practice he would repeat in 1907 – at a time when he was already established as the founding father of the psychoanalytic movement. By then, Freud had acknowledged certain professional mistakes – for example, he had come to regard his seduction theory (see page 56) as his 'first great error'. But drawing a line in the sand and moving on from perceived gaffes and blunders was a feature of his career – and something he ideally liked to do away from the gaze of the wider world.

It's All in
the Mind

'For we found, to our great surprise at first, that each
individual hysterical symptom immediately and
permanently disappeared when we had succeeded
in bringing clearly to light the memory of the
event by which it was provoked …'

SIGMUND FREUD AND JOSEF BREUER,
STUDIES ON HYSTERIA, 1895

By 1886 Freud was a married man and established in private practice. Among his patients were a number of mostly young Jewish women from the middle class exhibiting signs of neuroses (that is to say, for example, feelings of anxiety, obsessional thoughts, compulsive acts and other physical complaints with no clear physiological origin). A good many of them were sent his way by fellow physician and old university friend, Josef Breuer.

Up until this point, Freud had largely conformed to mechanist orthodoxy, seeking neurological explanations for neuroses and hysteria. Early published works, such as 1891's *On Aphasia* (on how damage to the brain can affect language use), speak of his commitment to this tradition. Yet as early as during his stint with Charcot, and partly because of his study there, Freud was toying with the idea that certain conditions had purely psychological causes – that is to say, they arose from the mind. For instance, Charcot did not believe that hypnosis could be used to treat hysteria but was merely a method to induce and examine its symptoms. Hysteria, he contended, was a neurological phenomenon. Freud, though, was open to the idea that it was a psychological one. Furthermore, against his mechanist traditions, he pondered looking for its possible psychological roots, only for Charcot – the arch mechanist – to steer him away from such research in favour of seeking out its neurological cause.

Having returned to Vienna from Paris in 1885 and buoyed by his contact with Breuer (who served as something of a father figure to him), which would continue over the next few years, Freud determined to follow up his interest in the possible psychological origins of nervous disorders. He became convinced, as well, that hypnosis could after all be used to treat cases of hysteria and

---

IT TAKES TWO

Breuer was a pivotal figure in the early period of Freud's career, during which Freud researched several different methods of exploring the mind. Indeed, it is fair to say that without Breuer, Freud might never have adopted the psychoanalytic technique. In 1907 Breuer would reflect on their in-depth discussions of the experiences of their (sometimes shared) patients: 'In this way our theoretical views grew up – not, of course, without divergences, but nevertheless in work that was so much carried out in common that it is really hard to say what came from one and what from the other.'

---

neurosis – a view bolstered by Breuer's reports of his treatment of his patient Anna O. in 1882 (see Case Study on page 36). Freud began to see neurosis and hysteria as symptoms of unconscious inhibitions. By focusing on the patient's psychological health and freeing their mind of inhibitions of which they were not even aware, he believed their neuroses could be cured.

The key, as the Anna O. case suggested to him, was to identify the index event that created a repressed memory, which manifested as hysteria. As he and Breuer would put it in *Studies on Hysteria*, 'when the patient had described that event in the greatest possible detail and had put the affect into words' their hysterical symptoms dissipated. 'Hysterics,' they concluded, 'suffer mainly from reminiscences.' Freud had always enjoyed the study of history (and indeed the accumulation of antiquities would become one of his few great non-professional passions) and now he started to view his role as that of an archaeologist of the mind. By excavating the patient's reminiscences, Freud believed he could transform 'hysterical misery into common unhappiness'.

To this end, Freud rejected altogether one of the most popular treatments of the day for nervous disorders – electrotherapy, in which electric currents were passed through the patient's body. He was in no doubt that this method, as he would later note, was 'of no help whatever'. Instead, he became an increasingly skilled practitioner of hypnosis (as Breuer had done before him). However, he soon grew frustrated with the mixed results that hypnosis delivered and so he developed a new 'pressure technique'.

Freud realized that successful treatment of neuroses and hysteria relied on the patient communicating the root cause of their problem even as they did not realize they were doing so. Hypnotism was merely one way to get them to talk without self-censorship. He considered that the pressure technique achieved the same result, but far more effectively. The process was simple. Using his hands, he applied pressure to his patient's forehead and asked them to relate 'whatever appeared before their inner eye or passed through their memory at the moment of pressure'. He was struck by the range of pictures, ideas and unconscious memories that were produced. If the first application of pressure yielded little, he found repeated applications usually produced the desired results.

One patient who received this treatment, in 1892, came to be identified as Elisabeth von R. She consulted him after enduring two years of leg pains but proved especially resistant to the pressure technique. Freud related in *Studies on Hysteria* how he confronted her in order to breach her psychological defences:

> I no longer accepted her declaration that nothing had occurred to her, but assured her that something must

have occurred to her. Perhaps, I said, she had not been sufficiently attentive, in which case I would be glad to repeat my pressure. Or perhaps she thought that her idea was not the right one. This, I told her, was not her affair; she was under an obligation to remain completely objective and say what had come into her head, whether it was appropriate or not. Finally, I declared that I knew very well that something had occurred to her and that she was concealing it from me; but she would never be free of her pains so long as she concealed anything. By thus insisting I brought it about that from that time forward my pressure on her head never failed in its effect.

Eventually, he told Elisabeth von R. that he believed her illness was the manifestation of the psychological anguish she felt as a result of falling in love with her brother-in-law. She utterly rejected his diagnosis but Freud stuck to his guns and reported that she was duly cured. Her treatment represented Freud's first tentative steps towards developing psychoanalysis. But he never forgot the major role Breuer and Anna O. played in its genesis. In 1909 he told a lecture audience: 'If it is a merit to have brought psychoanalysis into being, that merit is not mine. I had no share in its earliest beginnings.'

CASE STUDY: ANNA O

> 'The germ cell of the whole of psychoanalysis.'
>
> **JOSEF BREUER COMMENTING ON THE
> ANNA O. CASE, 1907**

Although Anna O. is the case study that effectively launched Freud's career, it is generally believed that he never actually met her himself but gained all his knowledge of the case second-hand from Breuer. Nonetheless, his analysis of her condition in conjunction with Breuer paved the way for what would become psychoanalysis. So who was Anna O. and why was her case so important?

Well, to begin with there never was an Anna O. – it was merely the pseudonym they chose to protect the identity of Bertha Pappenheim, who had been born in Vienna in 1859. When she was about twenty-one years old, her father fell seriously ill with tuberculosis and was confined to bed. Anna (which we shall call her, as Freud and Breuer intended) nursed him tirelessly but started to suffer symptoms of ill health herself (entirely unrelated to her father's condition) and so she came under Dr Breuer's care.

Up to this point in her life, Anna had been generally in very good health and was considered an intelligent girl with a good imagination. Yet her health deteriorated so starkly as she tended her father that she was eventually prevented from having any contact with him. He, meanwhile, lost his battle for survival in April of 1881.

Anna's symptoms were many and varied – some were seemingly unserious when taken in isolation, but as part of a broader picture they pointed to an individual in meltdown. She suffered coughing fits, alternating bouts of lethargy (usually in the afternoon and evening) and extreme excitability, paralysis in the limbs on her right side, and was sometimes unable to control her eye movements. She also developed problems with her vision and a squint. In addition, she took to sleepwalking and developed hydrophobia that rendered her unable to drink for days on end. Multilingual, she took to swapping between languages seemingly without realizing it and would sometime break a sentence mid-flow, repeating the last word before completing the sentence. As her mental state deteriorated, she was entirely unable to speak for a two-week period and also became bed-bound. To top it all, she was dogged by anxiety and endured appalling hallucinations so that she would awaken from daytime naps crying 'tormenting, tormenting'.

In short, there was plenty for Breuer to get his teeth into. He discerned four clear stages in the course of her decline and recovery. The first, which he called the 'latent incubation' period began in July 1880 and lasted into the December of that year. Although her symptoms were at a relatively low level, they were nonetheless clear to those who knew her well. Next came the period of 'manifest illness', when her symptoms were at their worst. A stuttering recovery was halted by the death of her father in April. Such was the concern that she might try to kill herself that in June she was moved from the family home in a multi-storey building to another, ostensibly safer property. Over the following months to December 1881, her condition was characterized by periods of seemingly normal behaviour and episodes of sleepwalking. The final phase, which lasted until June 1882, was one of gradual recovery under the guidance of Breuer.

Breuer discovered that one way to relieve her symptoms was to get her to describe her hallucinations under hypnotism – a process usually undertaken in the evening and after which she was generally more relaxed. Having diagnosed her with hysteria, these sessions provided Breuer with great insights into her state of mind. It soon became clear that many of the thoughts and hallucinations that caused her such distress directly correlated to her experiences of looking after her ailing father and to other unpleasant memories.

For instance, she described a vivid dream in which she was left paralysed and helpless as a black snake approached a bed-bound patient. The paralysis that afflicted Anna could thus be identified as a physical manifestation of the anxiety depicted in this dream. Similarly, Breuer was able to link her bouts of hydrophobia back to a childhood experience when she witnessed her grandmother's dog

– which she did not much like – taking a drink from a glass of water meant for her. So horrifying was this event in the young girl's life that other negative feelings and horrifying thoughts that she had in her adult life manifested themselves in her hydrophobia.

Breuer thus instigated what became known as the cathartic method – the recollection under hypnosis of a traumatic index event that produced a pathogenic memory, which in turn induced a particular physical symptom. Anna, meanwhile, referred to the method as 'talking therapy' and, somewhat wryly, as 'chimney sweeping'. As the root cause of each individual symptom was brought to Anna's conscious attention, the symptom itself would seemingly disappear. Over time she was completely cured and went on to live a full and productive life, although debate continues to rage as to just how big a contribution Breuer made to her recovery, given she never indicated how helpful she believed Breuer's work to have been.

Regaining Unconsciousness

'Properly speaking, the unconscious is the real psychic; its inner nature is just as unknown to us as the reality of the external world, and it is just as imperfectly reported to us through the data of consciousness as is the external world through the indications of our sensory organs.'

SIGMUND FREUD, *DREAM PSYCHOLOGY: PSYCHOANALYSIS FOR BEGINNERS* (1920)

Pivotal to everything Freud was doing is the concept of the unconscious (often also called the subconscious). While the notion has been comprehensively subsumed into our culture for a long while now, it was an idea only half-formed when Freud came on the scene. His attempts to analyse and understand the nature of the unconscious would fundamentally reposition our comprehension of ourselves and how we function within the wider world.

Given the complexity of the subject, it is little surprise that his conception of the unconscious changed and evolved throughout his long career. Nor, of course, was he the first person to recognize its existence. But while he freely acknowledged that he was building on the work of others, he was the first to win mainstream recognition for the subconscious as a scientific reality. As he reflected in 1926, when he reached his seventieth birthday, 'The poets and philosophers before me discovered the unconscious; what I discovered was the scientific method by which the unconscious can be studied.'

His own initial interest in the unconscious was doubtless prompted in part by interactions with one of his professors at the University of Vienna, Franz Brentano. A former Catholic priest who had struggled to accept the doctrine of papal infallibility, Brentano's most famous work was 1874's *Psychology from an Empirical Standpoint*, which set out possible models of the unconscious. Freud, though, took his work on several stages.

In Freud's first great formulation (as set out in *The Interpretation of Dreams* in 1899), the mind is divided into three distinct areas: the conscious, the preconscious and the unconscious.

- Conscious – that part of the mind taken to comprise those things of which we are aware, and that we may contemplate and discourse upon in a rational manner.
- Preconscious – made up of all those ideas and memories that are latent most of the time but which may easily become conscious. (Think, for instance, of your mobile phone number – a number that may not immediately roll off your tongue but which you can probably dredge up as required without too much effort.)
- Unconscious – those desires, impulses and wishes that are normally inaccessible to the conscious mind but which can significantly influence our behaviour.

It is an imagining of the mind that has commonly been illustrated using the so-called Iceberg Model. Just as only a small proportion of an iceberg is ever visible above the waterline, so in this model we 'see' only the conscious, while the vast majority of the mind (i.e. the preconscious and unconscious) goes 'unseen' beneath the waterline. It should be understood, however, that Freud's three-stage model does not reflect a physiological reality but is rather an academic tool for exploring the mind's functioning. As he wrote in his 1925 work, *An Autobiographical Study*:

> The subdivision is part of an attempt to picture the apparatus of the mind as being built up on a number of agencies or systems whose relations to one another are expressed in spatial terms, without, however, implying any connection with the actual anatomy of the brain. (I have described this as the topographical method of approach.)

According to his topographical model, the conscious and unconscious are in a fairly permanent state of conflict. In highly simplified terms, the unconscious is full of instinctive drives that often run up against what we know to be safe, civilized and socially acceptable behaviour in our conscious mind. The preconscious, meanwhile, serves as a sort of mediator between the two sides. In his *Introductory Lectures on Psychoanalysis* (1917), Freud characterized the ensuing struggle as follows:

Let us therefore compare the system of the unconscious to a large entrance hall, in which the mental impulses jostle one another like separate individuals. Adjoining this entrance hall there is a second, narrower room – a kind of drawing room – in which consciousness, too, resides. But on the threshold between these two rooms a watchman performs his function: he examines the different mental impulses, acts as a censor and will not admit them into the drawing room if they displease him ... The impulses in the entrance hall of the unconscious are out of sight of the conscious, which is in the other room; to begin with they must remain unconscious. If they have already pushed their way forward to the threshold and have been turned back by the watchman, then they are inadmissible to consciousness; we speak of them as repressed. But even the impulses which the watchman has allowed to cross the threshold are not on that account necessarily conscious as well; they can only become so if they succeed in catching the eye of consciousness. We are therefore justified in calling this second room the system of the preconscious.

Freud argued, as we shall see in greater detail later on, that the unconscious of each individual is driven in large part (though not exclusively) by the libido, which is defined by the development (healthy or otherwise) of sexual desires and instincts in early infancy. As we grow older and gain more experience of the external world, Freud said, the thoughts of the unconscious are repressed and censored if they are deemed contrary to the interests of the conscious. Nonetheless, the libido and other unconscious drives remain present and are released in a number of ways. For instance, they may manifest as physical symptoms (such as nervous conditions), in dreams, slips of the tongue (or, as they are sometimes called, Freudian slips) and jokes. Freud also suggested that it is the redirected sublimated energy of the sexual drive that underpins, for instance, humanity's creative and scientific endeavours and the very construction of civilizations. He suggested that another way to liberate the thoughts of the unconscious – and thus alleviate the potentially negative effects of their repression – is to subject oneself to psychoanalysis.

Yet Freud never lost sight of the fact that the true nature of the unconscious is fluid and elusive. In 1940 he called it 'as unknowable as electricity'. With this in mind, he repeatedly tweaked his topographical model, adding extra layers of complexity. For example, he came to believe that there were multiple forms of unconscious censorship, as well as additional types of instinct and further complications such as the concept of narcissism. Nonetheless, his three-stage model of the mind remains a good starting point for any student of Freud.

THE EGO, THE SUPEREGO AND THE ID

'We are warned by a proverb against serving two masters at the same time. The poor ego has things even worse: it serves three masters and does what it can to bring their claims and demands into harmony with one another … Its three tyrannical masters are the external world, the superego and the id.'

SIGMUND FREUD, *INTRODUCTORY LECTURES ON PSYCHOANALYSIS* (1936)

The most famous evolution of the topographical model came in 1923 when Freud published a paper called 'The Ego and the Id'. In this landmark work, he introduced the concepts of the *ego*, *superego* and *id*. Once more, these are theoretical constructs rather than physiological realities and have clear parallels with the topographical model.

The *id* (which broadly translates from the Latin as 'it') equates to the unconscious. The id is the seat of our needs and wants, and the home of the libido. Unguided by a moral compass of any sort, the id is the accumulation of the individual's instinctive drives and works in accordance with what Freud termed the pleasure principle. That is to say, the id seeks the immediate satisfaction of pleasure and, correspondingly, avoidance of pain.

As such, the young infant may be regarded as operating

virtually exclusively at the behest of the id. A newborn, for instance, always seeks immediate satisfaction of such basic cravings as hunger and thirst and, according to Freud, infantile sexual impulses. Writing in 1922, he described the id thus:

> It is the dark, inaccessible part of our personality ... a chaos, a cauldron full of seething excitations ... It is filled with energy reaching it from the instincts, but it has no organization, produces no collective will, but only a striving to bring about the satisfaction of the instinctual needs subject to the observance of the pleasure principle.

In *An Outline of Psychoanalysis*, published posthumously in 1940, he said, 'It contains everything that is inherited, that is present at birth, that is laid down in the constitution – above all therefore, the instincts, which originate from the somatic organization and which find a first physical expression here (in the id) in forms unknown to us.'

The id's counterpoint is the *superego* (*ego* translating from the Latin as 'I'). The superego may be seen as that self-critical, moralizing part of ourselves – our conscience, it can be said – which reflects the standards of wider society. These standards are introduced to us incrementally over time as we become more exposed to the outside world. This exposure begins with instruction from our parents and increases as we come into contact with other figures of authority, teachers and role models.

While the id informs us of what we want instinctively, the superego lays out the boundaries for what we may allow ourselves within the constructs of society. It is, therefore, responsible for such feelings as guilt, self-reproach, shame, weakness and duty. Since it begins with our evolving relationship to our parents, it was also regarded by Freud as a direct successor to the Oedipus complex (see page 96). In 1930, he described it thus: 'The superego is an authority that we postulate, and conscience a function that we ascribe to it – this function being to supervise and assess the actions and intentions of the ego, to exercise a kind of censorship.'

In between the id and the superego, the ego strives to act as mediator. While the word ego is today often used to denote a (commonly inflated) sense of self-esteem, it is a rather more nuanced concept within Freud's framework. There it serves as the basis of our conscious perception and intellectual functioning. It is, in other words, the home of our reason and common sense. Its role is multifaceted. It defends us by repressing the darker instincts of the id (something which it achieves subconsciously, somewhat ironically), and by compelling us to consider such ideas as safety, respectability and responsibility. It serves as a guide to the individual, encouraging us to adapt and evolve and to bridge the gap between the drives of our id and the demands of society imposed upon us by the superego to best fulfil our long-term interests.

As interaction with the world gradually reduces the dominance of the id in a child, the id is partially subsumed by the ego, which operates not in accordance with the pleasure principle but with what Freud called the Reality Principle. This privileges considerations of our long-term ability to function in society by tempering the desire for immediate gratification. Put in crude terms, it is why most of us, on wanting a new pair of shoes, opt to earn or save money to buy them rather than loot the shoe shop.

Yet as the quotation at the beginning of this section suggests, the well-intentioned ego has a tough job on its hands. While trying to rein in the id and moderate the feelings of anxiety, guilt and inadequacy inherent in the superego, it employs a variety of defence mechanisms including denial, displacement and repression. It is a constant battle, as any human knows, to maintain equilibrium between the many forces acting upon us, and Freud's model fully recognizes that fact.

Freud's description of the unconscious mind was one of those rare intellectual feats that genuinely changed the terms of reference for how we look at ourselves in a fundamental way. Nor was the extent of his achievement lost on him. In 1920, he wrote in *A General Introduction to Psychoanalysis*:

Humanity has in the course of time had to endure from the hands of science two great outrages upon its naive self-love [he was referring to the ideas of Copernicus and Darwin] … But man's craving for grandiosity is now suffering the third and most bitter blow from present-day psychological research which is endeavouring to prove to the ego of each one of us that he is not even master in his own house, but that he must remain content with the veriest scraps of information about what is going on unconsciously in his own mind. We psychoanalysts were neither the first nor the only ones to propose to mankind that they should look inward; but it appears to be our lot to advocate it most insistently and to support it by empirical evidence which touches every man closely.

Nobody Loves
You Like Yourself

'Whoever loves becomes humble. Those who love have,
so to speak, pawned a part of their narcissism.'

SIGMUND FREUD, 'ON NARCISSISM:
AN INTRODUCTION', 1914

In the work quoted above, Freud introduced a new component into his model of the human psyche – narcissism, or self-love. It became a key element in his interpretation of human behaviour (and in his eventual construction of the id–ego–superego model of the mind), although – in common with so many of his theories – it was and continues to be controversial.

Narcissism was a concept that he had been mulling over at least since the latter stages of the twentieth century's opening decade. Just as with the Oedipus complex, he looked to classical mythology to encapsulate the psychological state in question. According to Greek legend, Narcissus was a young boy who fell in love with his own reflection in a pool. Unable to tear himself from what was merely an image that could never reciprocate his love for it, he entered a spiral of despair and killed himself.

Freud delineated two distinct states of narcissism. The first, 'primary narcissism', may be viewed as a natural and normal state. He argued that since we are all born without a sense of self and other, primary narcissism in infancy is an expression of the coming together of the libidinal urge for pleasure and our inherent instinct for self-preservation. 'Loving oneself,' Freud wrote, is the 'libidinal complement to the egoism of the instinct of self-preservation.' As the child is exposed to the outside world and develops its ego, the phase of primary narcissism subsides.

In contrast, secondary narcissism results when the libido withdraws from objects external to the self and turns inwards. Although Freud considered secondary narcissism as a natural stage in development, he said that problems associated with transitioning out of it give rise to potential pathological conditions in adulthood such as megalomania and schizophrenia. Secondary narcissism may occur, for instance, if the outward object of an individual's affections (typically the mother in childhood) fails to replenish the subject's reserves of self-love (now directed outwards) with reciprocal love, care and affection.

Freud in due course investigated how narcissism impacts human relationships and our choice of love-objects. In *Civilization and Its Discontents*, he wrote:

If I love another person, he must in some way deserve it … He deserves it if, in certain important respects, he so much resembles me that in him I can love myself. He deserves it if he is so much more perfect than myself that in him I can love an ideal image of myself.'

Make Yourself
Comfortable

'When I set myself the task of bringing to light what human beings keep hidden with him … I thought the task was a harder one than it really is. He that has eyes to see and ears to hear may convince himself that no mortal can keep a secret. If his lips are silent, he chatters with his finger-tips; betrayal oozes out of him at every pore.'

SIGMUND FREUD, 1905

When Freud and Breuer published *Studies on Hysteria* in 1895, it tended to polarize fellow clinicians but made few ripples in the wider world. Nonetheless, it signposted Freud's fundamental change in direction. He was no longer a mechanist but believed that the symptoms of hysteria had psychical (that is to say, mental) roots. He was convinced that unconscious memories of traumatic events affected behaviour.

One of those scientists for whom Freud publicly expressed his esteem was the German physicist Hermann von Helmholtz (1821–94). Helmholtz made many notable contributions in a variety of fields but Freud was particularly interested in his theories of thermodynamics. Helmholtz held that energy could not be destroyed but instead transformed from state to state. Freud's evolving psychological model was based on a similar principle – psychic energy did not dissipate but when suppressed or driven from consciousness, it reappeared in a new form elsewhere. Hence energy suppressed in order to forget a trauma might reappear as a nervous twitch or some other physical symptom.

By 1896, however, cracks were beginning to show within the Freud–Breuer axis. In particular, Breuer was deeply uneasy at a series of papers his colleague delivered that year in which he suggested that hysteria and neuroses could almost invariably be traced back to a sexual cause. This notion was at the heart of what became known as Freud's 'seduction theory'. Reflecting on a broad, though hardly exhaustive, collection of case studies (thirteen in total), Freud noted that virtually all of the subjects had suffered incidents of sexual abuse that could be identified as the index event behind their symptoms. Furthermore, these incidents occurred in childhood, and generally when the patient had been under the age of four.

He concluded that repressed memories were virtually always linked to either the seduction or molestation of a child by an adult. He pointed an accusing finger in particular at nursemaids, governesses, domestic servants, teachers and tutors, while also acknowledging that older brothers were the perpetrators of abuse in several cases. (Freud would go on to accuse a nursemaid from his childhood as the 'prime originator' of his own neuroses, having been both 'my instructress in sexual matters' and notably impatient when he struggled to adapt to toilet training.) Episodes of abuse, he contended, were subsequently repressed by sufferers only to re-emerge as symptoms of neuroses post-puberty.

Many experts in the field were highly sceptical of this

new thesis, among them Breuer, who did not believe there was sufficient evidence to back up the claims – and contributed, as their beliefs diverged, to a general drifting apart of the two men. Before the decade was out, Freud had started to reject his own theory, having concluded that some of the incidents of abuse described to him by patients had been imagined. Controversially, modern scholarship suggests that several episodes only 'came to light' after Freud had exerted pressure on patients to bring their repressed memories to the surface, or else were the product of Freud's own interpretation of the patient's symptoms and utterances. Certainly, a good many of his own patients rejected the notion that they had been sexually abused in childhood.

Although Freud soon disregarded his seduction theory, he was now committed to treating mental disorders by examining the interaction of the conscious and unconscious regions of the mind. The seeds of the psychoanalytic movement were sown. Only its precise methodology remained to be established. The year 1896 is widely regarded as that in which psychoanalysis as we understand it now was born. It was that year that Freud coined the very term itself. It also marked the moment when he started experimenting with new techniques to encourage patients to talk and to break down resistance surrounding traumatic memories.

At this time, he stopped using the pressure technique and began to adopt the 'free association' method. This called for the patient to get into a relaxed frame of mind and then to share all their passing thoughts with the therapist, without any self-editing. The term 'free association' reflected how a thought or image might spontaneously lead to another thought or image without

COUCH THERAPY

By this time, Freud was also making a feature of the couch in his practice, and over time it would become the default emblem of the entire psychoanalytical movement. His first couch was in fact a Victorian daybed, gifted to him in 1890 by a grateful patient by the name of Madame Benvenisti. It had thus witnessed his dalliances with electrotherapy, hypnosis and the pressure technique but really proved its worth with his adoption of free association. It proved an ideal tool to encourage his patients to relax and allowed them to talk without having to make eye contact as would have been normal in a customary patient–doctor encounter. Indeed, he took to purposely positioning his own chair behind the couch, possibly after one female patient made a pass at him while on the couch (an occurrence, as we shall see, that was soon recognized as an occupational hazard for the psychoanalyst).

any clear logical progression. By talking freely in this way, it was hoped the patient would instinctively alert the therapist to damaging unconscious and repressed thoughts, free from the risk of the clinician guiding the patient's thoughts in any given direction. As Freud put it: 'Psychoanalysis was above all an art of interpretation.'

From his Vienna consulting room, Freud thus began an intellectual revolution – quietly at first, but soon to proclaim itself upon the international scene. Looking back on his career in 1937, he would comment:

Just as the archaeologist builds up the walls of the building from the foundations that have remained standing, determines the number and position of the columns from depressions, and reconstructs paintings from the remains found in the debris, so does the analyst proceed when he draws inferences from the fragments of memories, from the associations and from the behaviour of the subject of the analysis.

BREAK DOWN THE BARRIERS

'Psychoanalysis is like a woman who wants to be seduced but knows she will be underrated unless she offers resistance.'

SIGMUND FREUD, 'BEYOND THE PLEASURE PRINCIPLE', 1920

Freud sought to pick up on both verbal and non-verbal cues in order to unpick the sources of a patient's hysteria and neuroses. Over time he concluded that the mind adopted a number of key strategies in order to bury and repress unpleasant memories. Arguably the three most important of these were:

- Transference — a process whereby the patient unconsciously transfers their feelings for one subject towards another subject altogether.
- Projection – where the patient unconsciously insulates his or herself from their own urges and thoughts by denying their existence in themself and instead attributing them to someone else. Freud would in time come to believe that projection did not take place arbitrarily but adopted a subject in whom the patient could unconsciously detect some trace of the thoughts or feelings being projected. For instance, Subject A might accuse Subject B of harbouring a desire for Subject A's brother's wife, although in reality Subject A's own feelings for her are much stronger than the passing attraction felt by Subject B.
- Resistance — in which the patient fosters a mental block that forbids remembrance or acceptance of a particular event or thought. In other words, the ego erects a defence against a perceived threat. In practical terms, this might manifest as the patient's active non-cooperation with the doctor.

Freud recognized that it fell to the clinician to come up with methods (such as the free association technique) to overcome each and all of these potential sources of blockage that could derail recovery. However, transference held particular risks for the doctor as well as the patient, since he was in prime position to be the target of the patient's transference.

This could reveal itself in the patient fostering a romantic or erotic attachment to the therapist. For the patient, of course, the therapist might become something of a heroic figure, deciphering the cause of the patient's suffering and alleviating their symptoms – indeed, the patient could come to feel utterly dependent. Freud likely positioned his chair behind the patient's couch after just such an episode when a female patient attempted to make her apparent feelings of attraction known to him. Similarly, Anna O. came to believe that she was in love with Breuer during the several months of their association. Breuer never undertook such a prolonged and comprehensive treatment of a patient again (a fact that led him to pass several clients on to Freud instead) and it is highly probable that the extra burden of redirecting Anna's romantic sentiments contributed to his sense of exhaustion.

Yet a patient could just as easily redirect feelings of anger, resentment or mistrust. For example, one of Freud's most famous case studies, that of the Rat Man, included an episode where the subject flew into a mad rage with

Freud. But Freud saw that transference could be used as a tool to identify a source of neuroses, even while it seemed to serve as a barrier to therapy. This is because, he said, the neurotic repeats instead of remembering – that is to say, while the patient uses transference as a protection against traumatic thoughts, he is also playing out with the subject of the transference a conflict that can help identify the source of the trauma after all.

Doctor,
Heal Thyself

'His determination, courage and honesty made him
the first human being not merely to get glimpses of
his own unconscious mind – earlier pioneers had often
got as far as that – but actually to penetrate into and
explore its deepest depths. This imperishable
feat was to give him a unique position in history.'

ERNEST JONES, *THE LIFE AND WORK
OF SIGMUND FREUD*, 1953

Freud's father died in 1896, an event that had a significant impact on him – not least because he became acutely aware of his own neuroses. For example, he noted that he was having more bad dreams than before, experiencing low moods and more generalized emotional disturbance, and even suffering heart irregularities.

Realizing a correlation between these symptoms and his father's death, from 1897 until the end of the century Freud conducted a rigorous self-analysis. This involved an examination of his dreams and childhood memories, which could be challenging, exhausting, distressing and exhilarating. He shared many details of the experience in letters to Wilhelm Fliess. Fliess was a Berlin-based ear, nose and throat specialist who took Freud's most daring ideas seriously at a moment when others were less generous in their support. Indeed, Fliess had some fairly *outré* ideas of his own, including a theory that sexual illnesses derived from disturbances in the nasal mucous membranes (he would in due course operate twice on Freud's nose). The two began corresponding in

1893 and, after Freud's break with Breuer, Fliess became his leading professional confidante. The importance Freud attached to his self-analysis is summed up by his assertion to Fliess in 1897 that 'The chief patient I am preoccupied with is myself.' 'Some sad secrets of life are being tracked back to their first roots,' he wrote. 'I am now experiencing myself all the things that as a third party I have witnessed going on in my patients.'

Freud was characteristically courageous in confronting his demons, and much of the work that he carried out on himself fed directly into the publications that would propel him to stardom over the next few years. His uncompromising attitude to the job in hand is evident in his willingness to share his analysis of one particularly troubling dream that he had as a child. In it, he saw his mother – peacefully asleep – being carried into a room by a group of people sporting beaks, who then lay her on a bed. When Freud woke from the dream, he was crying and screaming and fled to his parents' bedroom.

His analysis went something like this. Owing to his keen interest in the ancient world, he had seen images of bird-headed people from Egyptian antiquity. A boy of his acquaintance had meanwhile told him that the word (in his native tongue of German) for bird served as a sexual slang term. Freud came to the conclusion that the apparent anxiety he had felt at the possibility of his mother's death was rather a disguise for his anxiety concerning the sexual feelings he harboured towards her (notably since an incident when, aged four, he stumbled upon his mother naked on the train journey from Leipzig to Vienna – a memory that lodged in his memory). Furthermore, he suggested the look of calm on her face in the dream was a transference of the expression his grandfather carried in his death throes, and that the dream contained elements of a death wish aimed towards his father.

As we shall see, this analysis would be more formally echoed in *The Interpretation of Dreams* and, specifically, in the formulation of the Oedipus complex. In time, Freud would make it a rule that members of the psychoanalytic movement should subject themselves to self-analysis just as he had done. As he wrote in *New Introductory Lectures on Psychoanalysis*:

> You can believe me when I tell you that we do not enjoy giving an impression of being members of a secret society and of practising a mystical science. Yet we have been obliged to recognize and express as our conviction that no one has a right to join in a discussion on psychoanalysis who has not had particular experiences which can only be obtained by being analysed oneself.

Dare to Dream

'The interpretation of dreams is the
royal road to a knowledge of the
unconscious activities of the mind.'

SIGMUND FREUD, *THE INTERPRETATION
OF DREAMS*, 1899

As he undertook his self-analysis, Freud began to write *The Interpretation of Dreams*, which he published in late 1899 (although the volume carried a publication date of 1900). To say its reception was lukewarm is something of an understatement – sales figures stayed defiantly below four figures for several years. Yet today it is the book for which he is probably best known – an accessible text that contains many of the fundamental tenets that underpinned Freud's own 'Copernican revolution'.

Freud liked to cite Plato's assertion that dreams are a source of self-knowledge and carry with them a therapeutic effect. Freud regarded them as both offering a glimpse of the past and opening a window on to the subconscious. Furthermore, he contended that the content of our dreams is not trivial – even though they may appear that way in the retelling – but point us towards the profound issues that occupy our unconscious mind. As he put it: 'Dreams are never concerned with trivialities; we do not allow our sleep to be disturbed by trifles.' He believed dreams allow us to safely address those thoughts and feelings that are too shameful or unsettling to confront in our conscious existence. 'All dreams are in a sense dreams of convenience,' he wrote. 'They serve the purpose of prolonging sleep instead of waking up. Dreams are the guardians of sleep and not its disturbers.'

So what made *The Interpretation of Dreams* such an important text? Most fundamentally, Freud became the first person to convincingly argue on (admittedly disputed) scientific grounds that dreams are a reflection of the unconscious – occurring as they do when we are in deep sleep and our conscious minds are resting. He also set out the first ground rules for the logical analysis of dreams, imposing some sort of order where disorder had previously flourished. In 1940's *An Outline of Psychoanalysis*, he acknowledged the perplexity of dreams with these words:

> Dreams, as everyone knows, may be confused, unintelligible or positively nonsensical. What they say may contradict all that we know of reality, and we behave in them like insane people, since, so long as we are dreaming, we attribute objective reality to the contents of the dream.

Freud considered that the observable content of

In *The Interpretation of Dreams*, Freud provided a two-part structural analysis, saying each dream consists of:

- Manifest contents – the events of the dream as recalled by the dreamer
- Latent content – unconscious ideas which lie hidden and coded behind the manifest content

dreams results from sensory experiences while asleep, combined with recent worries and concerns ('day residue'). The latent content, meanwhile, comprises repressed wishes from the subconscious that attach themselves to the manifest content in a disguised manner (a process known as 'dreamwork'). The two chief modes of disguising unconscious thought that Freud identified were condensation (where multiple ideas, objects and themes are brought together in a single object or person) and displacement (in which meaning is transferred to a different person, object or action). For instance, if you see a man being stabbed in front of a blue car, you may displace your fear of the assailant into a fear of blue cars. 'Dream displacement and dream condensation,' Freud said, 'are the two governing factors to whose activity we may ... ascribe the form assumed by dreams.'

He made other bold claims in the book too, perhaps most notably: 'When the work of interpretation has been completed, we perceive that a dream is the fulfilment of a wish.' He went on to explain: 'The more one is occupied with the solution of dreams, the readier one becomes to acknowledge that the majority of the dreams of adults deal with sexual material and give expression to erotic wishes.' One can easily imagine how such an argument played in drawing rooms across late-nineteenth-century Europe. But more of wish fulfilment and its sexual nature later.

Although *The Interpretation of Dreams* failed to set the world on fire at publication, Freud was quite convinced that he had lit the touchpaper for a revolution in the understanding of the human mind. In 1909 he looked back on how he felt after finishing the text: 'I had completed my life work … there was nothing more for me to do and … I might just as well lie down and die.' Before *The Interpretation of Dreams*, Freud's career had principally been concerned with studying abnormalities of the mind (hysteria, neuroses), but his engagement with dreams allowed him to extend his practice to exploration of the mind as a whole – both 'abnormal' and 'normal'. It was a keystone work in the development of psychoanalysis, which Freud described in 1925 as 'the starting point of a new, deeper science of the mind which would be … indispensable for the understanding of the normal'.

CASE STUDY: DORA

> 'Dreaming, in short, is one of the devices we employ to circumvent repression, one of the main methods of what may be called indirect representation in the mind.'
>
> SIGMUND FREUD, *DORA: FRAGMENT OF AN ANALYSIS OF A CASE OF HYSTERIA*, 1905

Peter Gay, one of Freud's biographers, said that *The Interpretation of Dreams* is 'about more than dreams. It is an autobiography at once candid and canny, as tantalizing in what it omits as in what it discloses.' Indeed, Freud does allow the reader some access to his own dream landscape within its pages. For instance, he recalls a dream (or rather a fragment from the longer 'Count Thun' dream) in which he finds himself at a railway station, wearing some sort of disguise and in the company of an elderly blind (or partially blind) gentleman. Freud hands the man a glass urinal and the man subsequently urinates in front of him.

At that moment in the dream, Freud awoke, himself needing to go to the toilet. He analyses the dream as being concerned with an episode that occurred when he was seven or eight years old. His failure to correctly use a chamber pot had led his father, Jacob, to tell his mother that the boy would never amount to anything

– an assertion Freud overheard. The blindness in the dream, meanwhile, related to Jacob's severe eye problems, as well as Freud's part in promoting the use of cocaine in ophthalmic operations. As for the instance of public urination, it rendered the father figure in a position of shame and defencelessness, similar to that experienced by Freud at the hand of his father all those years before. Thus Freud turns his own life and dreams into material for his study.

However, some of his most famous dream analyses came in a series of case studies published in the years after *The Interpretation of Dreams*. The first, that concerning a subject known as Dora, appeared in 1905. Her case led Freud to observe: 'Those who have eyes to see and ears to hear will soon convince themselves that mortals cannot hide any secret.'

Dora (her real name was Ida Bauer) came to Freud in 1900 as an eighteen year-old suffering from hysteria. She displayed a number of symptoms, including coughing, amnesia, migraines, blackouts and depression. Her father brought her to Freud, having himself been under his medical care. She spent a total of eleven weeks in analysis with the doctor, whereupon she broke off the consultation having rejected key elements of Freud's diagnosis.

Dora lived with her parents, who endured a loveless marriage. The pair did, however, have a close relationship with another couple, referred to as Herr and Frau K.

Dora's father had suffered significant ill health and Frau K took on some of his care. While Dora personally liked Frau K, she began to suspect an affair with her father. Dora, meanwhile, accused Herr K of making sexual advances towards her – a charge he rejected and which her father seemed to doubt too. Freud initially reserved judgement on this question as well, although Dora would confide that she felt her father did not want to prohibit Herr K's access to her for fear of upsetting his own arrangement with Frau K.

Dora also reported a recurring dream to Freud in which her father awoke her suddenly as their house was ablaze. Her mother refused to abandon the property until she had found her jewellery box, to the fury of her father who wanted to effect an immediate escape with Dora and her sibling. On one level, Freud detected an unconscious fear related to Dora's cousins' reported habit of lighting matches, and her mother's insistence on locking a dining-room door that blocked a potential escape route. However, he also believed that her father in the dream was actually also portraying a representation of Herr K in a classic case of displacement. Dora's panic at her sudden rousing by him thus becomes a reflection of her fears of Herr K's advances. Herr K had previously given Dora a jewellery box, a term that was used colloquially at the time to denote the female genitalia. The protection of the 'jewellery box' from the passions implicit in the inferno, and her father's refusal to imperil the family to rescue it, thus took on new symbolic meaning for Freud.

His assertion to Dora that she harboured a repressed desire for both her father and Herr K, along with a combination of jealousy and desire towards Frau K, did not sit well with Dora and she chose to cease therapy. However, Freud reported that she returned to him two years later and told him that she had subsequently confronted the Ks and her symptoms had subsided. While Freud recognized failings (Dora didn't feel herself cured) in his treatment of the young woman, Dora's case was another landmark in the progression of his skills as an interpreter of dreams.

You Get What
You Wish For

'I do not know myself what animals dream of.
But a proverb ... does claim to know. 'What,' asks
the proverb, 'do geese dream of?' And it replies:
'Of maize.' The whole theory that dreams are wish
fulfilments is contained in these two phrases.'

SIGMUND FREUD, *THE INTERPRETATION
OF DREAMS*, 1899

The 'purpose' of dreams had long been debated – are they prophecies of events to come, reflections of the recent past, problem-solving exercises or something else entirely? No one had hitherto come up with much of an evidential basis to justify any of these – or many other – suggestions. Hence, Freud's insistence that dreams provide wish fulfilment was dramatic and impactful, while his suggestion that they were mostly wishes of a sexual nature was nothing less than scandalous. He also noted: 'In dream interpretation this importance of the sexual complexes must never be forgotten, though one must not, of course, exaggerate it to the exclusion of all other factors.' A dream of his own set him on the path to the theory of dreams as wish fulfilment and it was notably not sexual in nature.

Freud had the 'dream of Irma's injection' in 1895 and it was the first dream he subjected to rigorous interpretation, although he conceded that there remained gaps in his analysis. In real life, Irma was a patient of Freud's during the summer of 1895. She had rejected a particular course of treatment that he had suggested for her and though her health improved, some symptoms persisted. On the day before the night of his dream, Freud had been told by a colleague that Irma was 'better, but not quite well'.

Freud described his dream thus:

A large hall – numerous guests, whom we were receiving. Among them was Irma. I at once took her to one side, as though to answer her letter and to reproach her for not having accepted my 'solution' yet. I said to her, 'If you still get pains, it's really only your fault.' She replies, 'If you only knew what pains I've got now in my throat and stomach and abdomen – it's choking me.' I was alarmed and looked at her. She looked pale and puffy. I thought to myself that after all I must be missing some organic trouble. I took her to the window and looked down her throat … She then opened her mouth properly and on the right I found a big white patch; at another place I saw extensive whitish grey scabs upon some remarkable curly structures which were evidently modelled on the turbinal bones of the nose. I at once called in Dr M, and he repeated the examination and confirmed it … 'There's no doubt it's an infection, but no matter; dysentery will supervene and the toxin will be eliminated' … We were directly aware, too, of the origin of the infection. Not long before, when she was feeling unwell, my friend Otto had given her an injection … (and I saw before me the formula for this printed in heavy type) … Injections of this sort ought not to be given so thoughtlessly … And probably the syringe had not been clean.

Freud noted down the details of this dream as soon as he woke. It was clear that his exchange with the colleague the previous day served as a jumping-off point for the dream but he now sought to explore its many details and relate them to his own subconscious thoughts. The white scab on the turbinal bone, for example, he linked to an illness his daughter had suffered from and to concerns he had about his own health. He also recounted failures in his medical career, including an incident where a patient reacted badly to one of his prescriptions and he was forced to call on a more experienced colleague for help. He thus saw his dream as a means to critique his own abilities as a clinician but, crucially, also to relieve himself of the guilt he then felt for the failure to fully remedy Irma's ailments. He wished to absolve himself of responsibility and the dream allowed him to do just that.

What do geese dream of? Of maize. What did Freud dream of? He wished to make his patients better, not worse.

A Cigar is Not Just a Cigar

'Dreams, then, are often most profound when they seem most crazy. In every epoch of history, those who have had something to say but could not say it without peril have eagerly assumed a fool's cap.'

SIGMUND FREUD, *THE INTERPRETATION OF DREAMS*, 1899

Freud's claim to be able to comprehend the underlying nature of dreams relied in no small part on his intricate interpretation of their signs and symbols. Something which appeared in the manifest content of a dream – even if nothing more than an apparently innocuous detail – might hold the key to unlocking the dreamer's latent thoughts.

Yet while Freudian symbols were vital to his theories of the unconscious, they were also ripe for mockery by non-believers. Not least because the process of interpretation was – and is – by its nature hugely subjective and frequently discomforting (especially in its often stark sexual content). *The Interpretation of Dreams* is full of Freud's guidelines on how to decode dream symbols. For instance:

It is perfectly true that dreams contain symbolizations of bodily organs and functions, that water in a dream often points to a urinary stimulus, and that the male genitals can be represented by an upright stick or a pillar, and so on.

Or:

Boxes, cases, chests, cupboards and ovens represent the uterus, and also hollow objects, ships, and vessels of all kind.

Or:

To represent castration symbolically, the dreamwork makes use of baldness, hair-cutting, falling out of teeth and decapitation. If one of the ordinary symbols for a penis occurs in a dream doubled or multiplied, it is to be regarded as a warding-off of castration.

Other symbols could be more opaque in their meaning. In one passage of the book, he told the story of a Jewish woman who dreamt that a stranger handed her a comb. Just prior to the dream, the woman had violently argued with her mother over her plans to marry a Christian suitor. When Freud asked her what associations were conjured up by the comb, the woman recalled an incident from childhood when her mother had chastised her for picking up a stranger's comb, warning that to use it risked 'mixing the breed'. So it was that the comb emerged as a symbol of the woman's fear of arousing disapproval by marrying outside her religion.

One of Freud's most complicated interpretations was that of Wolf Man, whose case he took on in 1910. Wolf

A Cigar is Not Just a Cigar

Man was in fact a Russian aristocrat in his early twenties called Sergei Pankeieff, and he was almost incapacitated by psychiatric problems. He received his pseudonym from Freud on account of the following recurring dream that he related (as documented by Freud in *From the History of an Infantile Neurosis*, 1918):

> I dreamed that it was night and I was lying in my bed. Suddenly the window opened of its own accord, and I was terrified to see that some white wolves were sitting on the big walnut tree in front of the window. There were six or seven of them. The wolves were quite white, and looked more like foxes or sheepdogs, for they had big tails like foxes and they had their ears pricked like dogs when they pay attention to something. In great terror, evidently of being eaten up by the wolves, I screamed and woke up.

Freud believed this dream, which Wolf Man had had since he was about four, provided the way to identifying the source of Wolf Man's neuroses. The long tails, for instance, he interpreted as being related to the boy's childhood fear of castration. The wolves themselves were symbolic of the boy's father, and their stillness conversely representative of violent movement. It turned out that, as a two year-old, Wolf Man had woken from an afternoon nap to witness his parents in the course of vigorous lovemaking – a sight that filled him with terror and manifested itself in a lifelong fear of wolves. This is, of course, a greatly condensed synopsis of Freud's very detailed analysis, but serves to show how the interpretation of dreams and the symbols within them became crucial to his therapeutic practice.

Nonetheless, he was well aware that the desire to read meaning into anything and everything was a danger – both to accurate diagnosis and to the credibility of psychoanalysis as a whole. The observation that 'Sometimes a cigar is just a cigar' (in other words, that it is not necessarily a phallic symbol) has been regularly attributed to the famously cigar-loving Freud, although it is almost certainly apocryphal. However, he echoed the sentiment when one of his patients related a dream in which she held a wriggling fish in her hand. She confidently proclaimed to Freud that it surely represented a penis. Freud countered that her mother, a keen astrologer born under the sign of Pisces, had made clear her opposition to her daughter's appointments with him, so the fish more likely represented her. Sometimes a fish is just a fish … or a matriarch … but not a penis.

Sex is
Everywhere

'The more I set about looking for such disturbances
– bearing in mind the fact that everyone hides the
truth in matters of sex – and the more skilful I became
at pursuing my enquiries in the face of a preliminary
denial, the more regularly was I able to discover
pathogenic factors in sexual life.'

SIGMUND FREUD, 1907

Despite Freud's acknowledgement that other factors ought to be considered in psychoanalysis beyond those of a sexual nature, his name quickly became synonymous with sex and has remained so ever since. The musicologist (and father of Little Hans) Max Graf was moved to note that in Viennese circles '… he was the man who saw sex in everything. It was considered bad taste to bring up Freud's name in the presence of ladies.'

Freud's focus on the sexual origins of hysteria was also the primary cause of his split with Breuer in the 1890s and was a prominent theme in his correspondence with Fliess over the years that followed. Consider, for example, his observation in 1897:

The insight has dawned on me that masturbation is the one major habit, the 'primary addiction', and it is only as a substitute and replacement for it that the other addictions – to alcohol, morphine, tobacco and the like – come into existence.

By 1905 he was telling American neurologist James Putnam (with a nudge and a wink):

> Sexual morality as defined by society, in its most extreme form that of America, strikes me as very contemptible. I stand for an infinitely freer sexual life, although I myself have made very little use of such freedom. Only so far as I considered myself entitled to.

While in 1908 he wrote in '"Civilized" Sexual Morality and Modern Nervous Illness':

> If a man is energetic in winning the object of his love, we are confident that he will pursue his other aims with an equally unswerving energy; but if, for all sorts of reasons, he refrains from satisfying his strong sexual instincts, his behaviour will be conciliatory and resigned rather than vigorous in other spheres of life as well.

Reflecting on his bitter split with Freud some fifty years earlier, Carl Jung recalled in 1962: 'There was no mistaking the fact that Freud was emotionally involved in his sexual theory to an extraordinary degree ... he was a great man, and what is more, a man in the grip of his daimon.'

Arguably the work that cemented Freud's reputation as 'the sexpert' was his *Three Essays on the Theory of*

Sexuality, published in 1905. This was, he considered, his greatest work alongside *The Interpretation of Dreams*. Here he laid out his overarching theory of human sexuality, especially in relation to childhood – a subject, as we might expect, that provoked uproar among the turn-of-the-century crowd.

The first of the three essays was entitled 'The Sexual Aberrations', in which he examined the nature of sexual perversion and drew a distinction between the *sexual object* (by which he meant the subject of sexual attraction) and the *sexual aim* (the act to which the sexual drive aspires). He characterized the 'normal' sexual aim as 'the union of the genitals in the act known as copulation, which leads to a release of the sexual tension and a temporary extinction of the sexual instinct – a satisfaction analogous to the sating of hunger'. He then contended with such delicate subjects as paedophilia and bestiality (noting that though deemed perversions of the insane, they were evident in 'normal' people as well), and homosexuality. The origins of perceived perversions were, he concluded predictably, rooted in the subjects' childhood experiences.

The second essay, 'Infantile Sexuality', attempted to analyse the sexual development of children from birth and to investigate how psychosexual development progresses into adulthood. It was a truly shocking work for its time, when childhood innocence was not merely revered but sanctified. Freud revised this essay considerably over the decade and more following first publication, and it is considered in more depth in the next section.

The final essay, meanwhile, was 'The Transformations of Puberty', which sought to track the progress from infantile sexuality towards adult sexuality as characterized by the goal of sexual intercourse.

By the time the essays had gone through multiple revisions into the 1920s, the collected volume had grown in length by about 50 per cent. By then, it seemed less concerned with the differences between childhood and adult sexuality than in tracing the path that Freud considered led inexorably from one to the other.

THE KEY STAGES OF SEXUALITY

'No one who has seen a baby sinking back satiated from the breast and falling asleep with flushed cheeks and a blissful smile can escape the reflection that this picture persists as a prototype of the expression of sexual satisfaction in later life.'

SIGMUND FREUD, *THREE ESSAYS ON THE THEORY OF SEXUALITY: INFANTILE SEXUALITY*, 1905

Freud's theories of psychosexual development are so striking and shocking because they confront us with the idea that human sexuality evolves from the moment we are born. Indeed, he argued that the fact that human sexual life occurs in two distinct waves – in infancy and then at puberty and into adulthood – sets us apart from the animals. In a society that was accustomed to the idea that sexuality only reared its head from puberty (and, by extension, that the souls and minds of younger children were untainted by such base desires) and that 'decent people' ought to be able to wield control over their sexual urges, Freud represented a grave threat to accepted social norms. The quotation above gives a sense of the challenging discourse he adopted.

But redefining 'normal' was the hallmark of his career, and never less so than in relation to sexuality. For example, he undermined the idea that there is a naturally fixed object of the sex drive (namely, heterosexual genital intercourse), which raised the prospect that homosexuality and bisexuality naturally resulted from particular paths of infantile sexual development rather than, as was often argued, from physiological defects or moral decrepitude. Furthermore, he argued that neuroses and other forms of mental disorder typically resulted from anxiety caused in any given phase of sexual development.

At the heart of his model of sexual development was the notion that we are born with libido (the basic sexual drive). He contended that humans are born 'polymorphous perverse', which is to say that an infant to the age of five or six is able to derive sexual pleasure from any part of the body (having not yet been subjected to the process of socialization that privileges heterosexual, genital-focused desire). Freud configured a standard five-stage model of sexual development, in which different erogenous zones become the focal point of sexual pleasure. He argued that frustration or 'failure' related to any given phase (for instance, attracting the criticism of parents – especially – or other social entities in relation to the specific erogenous zone) might lead to a fixation on that particular zone, which in turn could manifest as adult neuroses. For instance, excessive parental strictness when toilet-training in the 'anal phase' might result in the child developing a compulsive personality in relation to cleanliness or neatness – the 'anal-retentive' of modern popular folklore. So what were the five phases Freud outlined?

• The oral stage – lasting roughly for the first year of the infant's life, during which the mouth is the primary means of satisfying libidinal urges. This is exemplified by the action of breastfeeding but also by the insertion of other objects into the mouth. At this stage, the child is dominated by the id but the ego develops as the child realizes it possesses its own body, distinct from the surrounding world. The process of weaning teaches the child self-awareness (not least as it comprehends its limited control over its environment) and also fosters the idea of delayed gratification, which in turn promotes the adoption of strategies (such as crying) to bring about gratification (for example feeding at the breast).

- The anal stage – experienced from about eighteen months to three years of age, when the focal erogenous zone moves from the mouth to the anus. Toilet-training is a key aspect in this phase, in which the id (and the desire for immediate relief and gratification) comes into conflict with the ego (as the social demand for orderly elimination of the body's waste necessitates further acceptance of delayed gratification). As Freud wrote in 1912: 'The excremental is all too intimately and inseparably bound up with the sexual; the position of the genitals – *inter urinas et faeces* – remains the decisive and unchangeable factor. One might say here, varying a well-known saying of the great Napoleon: "Anatomy is destiny."'

- The phallic stage – lasting between three and six years of age, where the genitalia become the principle erogenous zone. In this phase, children become increasingly aware of the characteristics of their own body and those of others and establish the physical differences between male and female bodies, as well as differing gender expectations. This stage is characterized by what Freud christened the Oedipus complex, one of his most famous and enduringly controversial ideas, looked at in more detail in the section on page 96.

- The latency stage – approximately from the ages of six to twelve, in which the unfettered urges of the id are hidden from the ego, and the superego undergoes a period of intensive development. The child now begins to behave much more in line with the moral codes provided by its parents and other sources of authority. Libidinal urges are directed towards other forms of socially acceptable gratification, such as hobbies and the development of friendships.

• The genital stage – the fifth and final stage that spans from puberty into adulthood, in which identifiable sexual urges (focused on the genital) reappear, but this time (unlike in the phallic stage) moderated by the ego and superego. Freud believed that in a fully navigated process of sexual development, the adult establishes psychological independence from the parents and can engage in a socially 'appropriate' adult sex life, usually centred on heterosexual relations and a desire to procreate.

Freud posited that the incomplete resolution of any particular stage of development may lead not only to neuroses but to 'perversions' as well – for instance, voyeurism, exhibitionism or fetishism. His theories regarding homosexuality and bisexuality, meanwhile, were incomplete by his own admission but he argued, for instance, that homosexuality may be seen in terms of inversion of sexual desire on to the self.

Freud employed his radical theories in one of his most famous case studies – Rat Man. The subject was one Ernst Lanzer, a lawyer in his late twenties who had suffered various obsessional neuroses for many years. However, his symptoms had got worse in the period leading up to him consulting Freud in 1907 (treatment lasted for a total of about six months). Lanzer suffered an array of compulsions including a desire to cut his own throat with a razor. His fears, though, were principally concerned with the well-being of a young woman (who would in due course become his wife) and his father (who had already been dead for several years – the resultant irrationality of his concern for his father was not lost on Rat Man). In particular, he became obsessed with the idea that these two people so dear to him would suffer a gruesome form of torture that he had heard about from a fellow army officer. This officer told him of a practice supposedly originating in China that involved strapping a pot of rats to the buttocks of the victim and leaving the rats to eat their way out to freedom.

Over time, Freud built up a complex picture of the interplay between the psychological defence mechanisms and symbolic and verbal associations underlying his patient's fears. He suggested Rat Man's neuroses were rooted in his sexual experiences in childhood. In particular, he believed that Rat Man's childish fear that his father would punish him for his early sexual adventures (including masturbation and the exploration of sexual curiosity he felt for his governess) had forged an indelible connection between sexual pleasure and guilt.

Fearing punishment for himself, he transposed it on to his wife-to-be, while his unacknowledged resentment of his father translated into a fear that something terrible would befall him (even though bizarrely – in the form of death – it already had). Thus with reference to his theory of infantile sexual development, Freud sought to solve Rat Man's neuroses. The story, however, did not ultimately have a happy ending – as Freud later noted, 'the patient's mental health was restored to him by the analysis' but 'like so many young men of value and promise, he perished in the Great War'.

Today, much of Freud's work of psychosexual development is treated with caution by experts in the field. It is doubtless an incomplete story and in certain respects – as in the treatment of homosexuality – reflects values of his own time even as he seemed to throw them into doubt. Nonetheless, while much of the detail of his theories in this area may have been discredited in the century or so since Freud unleashed them on the world, they continue to make us look at how we – as complex, confusing individuals – evolve our personalities and psychological make-up.

The Oedipus Complex

'In the second half of childhood a change sets in in the boy's relation to his father – a change whose importance cannot be exaggerated … He finds that his father is no longer the mightiest, wisest and richest of beings; he grows dissatisfied with him, he learns to criticize him and to estimate his place in society; and then, as a rule, he makes him pay heavily for the disappointment that has been caused him … he becomes a model not only to imitate but also to get rid of, in order to take his place.'

SIGMUND FREUD, 'SOME REFLECTIONS ON SCHOOLBOY PSYCHOLOGY', 1914

Of all Freud's many challenging ideas, few if any have embedded themselves into the popular mind as comprehensively as the Oedipus complex, despite having been long since widely debunked by subsequent theoreticians. In brief, it relates to the idea that all children in the phallic phase of sexual development have unconscious sexual desire for the parent of the opposite sex and a wish to exclude the parent of the same sex. The complicated emotions surrounding these wishes need to be fully resolved within the context of sexual development so as not to cause psychological issues later on. The latent phase, meanwhile, begins with the repression of the complex.

Freud looked to Greek mythology to frame the theory, seizing upon the story of Oedipus, king of the city-state of Thebes. He was the son of King Laius and his queen, Jocasta, and the troubles began when Laius turned to the famed Oracle at Delphi to discover if he and Jocasta would ever be blessed with children. The Oracle prophesied that they would have a son, but that he would kill Laius and marry Jocasta – not the answer the king had hoped for at all. When Jocasta fell pregnant and gave birth to a boy, Laius had the child's ankles pierced (Oedipus meaning *swollen foot*) and asked a shepherd to take the boy into the mountains and leave him there to die.

The shepherd, however, could not carry out the request. Oedipus eventually found himself at the court of the childless King Polybus and Queen Merope of Corinth, who chose to adopt him. On reaching adulthood, Oedipus learned that Polybus might not be his father. He then received a prophecy of his own from Delphi that he would kill his father and marry his mother. Believing this referred to Polybus and Merope, he decided not to return to Corinth, instead heading for Thebes.

On his journey there, he fell into dispute with a charioteer coming the other way and a brawl ensued, during which Oedipus killed the charioteer and his master, Laius. Part one of the Oracle's prophecy had thus come to pass. A while later, Oedipus encountered the Sphinx, which had been terrorizing Thebes and killing those who could not answer its riddle. However, Oedipus solved the conundrum and the Sphinx was killed. When he arrived in Thebes, Oedipus was received as a hero by Jocasta and her brother, Creon, who had temporarily assumed the crown in place of Laius. He told Oedipus that the killer of the Sphinx should have Jocasta's hand in marriage and the throne of Thebes. Thus the prophecy was completed.

Oedipus had four children with his own mother. Several years later, however, Thebes was overrun by disease. The trusty Oracle was called upon again, this time telling Creon that the city's misfortune was the result of the failure to bring Laius's killer to justice. Under duress, the blind prophet Tiresias revealed to Oedipus that he was Laius's killer. Oedipus rejected the story, instead claiming that Creon was plotting to seize power from him. However, further investigations proved to Oedipus that Tiresias was telling the truth. When Jocasta realized that her husband was in fact the child whom she thought had died decades earlier, she hanged herself. Oedipus, meanwhile, took two pins from her dress and gouged out his eyes. Blinded and cast into exile, Oedipus was succeeded as king by his uncle and brother-in-law, Creon.

Freud believed that the Oedipus complex applied to children of both sexes, although he acknowledged different aspects to the gendered experiences. Freud said that the boy, wishing to possess his mother, desires to remove his father as a rival. However, he fears the father's revenge were he to find out his feelings. Indeed, he suspects the father would take away that which the child loves most in this phase – his penis. Hence, the boy develops 'castration anxiety'. In 'normal' development, he sets out to remedy this anxiety by aping and assimilating father-like behaviours, so prompting a crucial episode in the development of his masculine identity. Moreover, his mother is gradually replaced as the target of his sexual impulses by women in general so as to avoid trauma.

Freud's theory about the complex for girls, meanwhile, evolved significantly over the years, but was far less satisfactory even to his most ardent followers. According to Freud, girls initially desire their mothers just as boys do. But on realizing that she does not possess a penis, she develops 'penis envy'. Yearning for a penis, her sexual desire transfers from mother to father, assisted by resentment that her mother has failed to 'equip' her with the said appendage. Desiring her father and wishing to eliminate her prime rival for his affections – her mother – the girl adopts and mimics the mother's behaviour. But fearing the loss of her mother's love, she represses the feelings of tension and resentment between mother and daughter. The girl thus begins to develop a mature, gendered sexual identity of her own; her sexual feelings for her father are repressed and replaced with feelings for men in general, while her wish for a penis is subsumed by her desire for a baby.

Tracing the genesis of his Oedipal theories has kept academics in work for years. One might look to the extraordinarily close relationship Freud had with his own mother (characterized by her adoration for 'my golden Sigi') and the complicated relations with his father, whose struggles to keep the family financially afloat and whose weakness in the face of an anti-Semitic

THE ELECTRA COMPLEX

Freud's one-time disciple, Jung, termed the phenomenon in girls the 'Electra' complex – named in honour of another figure from Greek mythology, the daughter of Agamemnon who incited her brother, Orestes, to kill their mother Clytemnestra and her lover, Aegisthus, in revenge for the murder of their father. Freud, however, never accepted the term, believing that it drew too close and inappropriate an analogy with the male Oedipal experience. For children of either sex, the ability to identify with the same-sex parent was considered by Freud a successful resolution of the complex. Among the potential results of non-resolution, he variously suggested mother- or father-fixations, neuroses, homosexuality and paedophilia.

assault likely fuelled the son's resentment towards him. Freud also once described his father to Fliess as 'one of these perverts ... responsible for the hysteria of my brother ... and those of several younger sisters', although the implication that Jacob abused his children cannot be verified. Nonetheless, by 1897, Freud was openly alluding to the experience of Oedipus, having recently lost his father and then seen a production of Sophocles's *Oedipus Rex*. He wrote to Fliess that year: 'I found in myself a constant love for my mother, and jealousy of my father. I now consider this to be a universal event in early childhood.'

In *The Interpretation of Dreams*, he wrote of Oedipus:

His destiny moves us only because it might have been ours – because the Oracle laid the same curse upon us before our birth as upon him. It is the fate of all of us, perhaps, to direct our first sexual impulse towards our mother and our first hatred and our first murderous wish against our father. Our dreams convince us that this is so.

However, it would not be until 1910 that Freud coined the term 'Oedipus complex', which he identified as the root cause of all neuroses. He would continue to revise and re-evaluate the theory all the way until his death in 1938, especially in reference to the feminine experience.

CASE STUDY: LITTLE HANS

'These were tendencies in Hans which had already been suppressed and which, so far as we can tell, had never been able to find uninhibited expression: hostile and jealous feelings against his father, and sadistic impulses (premonitions, as it were, of copulation) towards his mother.'

SIGMUND FREUD, 'ANALYSIS OF A PHOBIA IN A FIVE-YEAR-OLD BOY', 1909

The Oedipus Complex

While the theory of the Oedipus complex went through many years of evolution, the single most important case in its support was one that Freud took on in 1909 – a year before he introduced the term itself into public discourse. Little Hans was the pseudonym of Herbert Graf, the son of writer and critic Max Graf, a close friend of Freud's.

When Max brought his son to Freud, Hans was five years old. By this stage he had developed a profound phobia of horses – the symptom Freud was charged with treating. However, Freud saw the case less as a chance to offer a cure for the phobia than to study its causes. By this stage, he was already well advanced in formulating his ideas on the Oedipus complex and Hans offered the perfect opportunity to test out his hypotheses. Graf seems to have been quite happy for his son to be used in the interests of Freud's wider cause. In fact, Freud only sporadically saw Little Hans in person. Instead he worked mostly through correspondence with Hans' father, who was himself a supporter of Freud's theories. Indeed, he wrote to Freud in the first instance because he suspected that Hans presented a case that might be of interest. Freud suggested possible lines of questioning which the father could try with his son, and the father duly reported back what transpired.

Graf described the initial problem: 'He is afraid a horse will bite him in the street, and this fear seems somehow connected with his having been frightened by a large penis.' For Little Hans, this was a real problem, since the Graf's lived in a house opposite a coaching inn. There were always horses about and Hans no longer wished to leave the safety of his own home. On one occasion, while out with his nurse, he had witnessed a horse pulling a heavily laden bus when it collapsed and died. Hans particularly remembered its hooves clattering against the cobbled street.

Other selected points of interest about the case included:

- Hans had shown great interest in his penis (which he referred to as his 'widdler'), which had prompted admonitions from his mother. He had also had dreams involving babies' bottoms being wiped.
- Hans admitted to feeling jealous of his sister.
- He was particularly fearful of horses that had black markings around their mouths and that wore blinkers.
- He recalled once seeing a girl being told not to touch a white horse.
- He reported a dream involving giraffes.

Freud quickly diagnosed an Oedipus complex. The boy's interest in matters of the genitals and anus was a reflection of the sexual urges he was feeling in line with the early stages of sexual development, which included desire directed towards the mother. His resentment of his sister (he had hoped she might drown in the bath) was evidence for Freud that Hans did not wish to share his mother's attentions. The blinkered horses with black on their faces, meanwhile, correlated to his father, who wore glasses and sported a black moustache. The girl told not to touch the horse echoed his being told off for touching his penis (which on one occasion his mother had said would result in her sending for someone to chop it off, fuelling the child's castration fears).

Graf noted the details of his son's giraffe dream thus: 'In the night there was a big giraffe in the room and a crumpled one: and the big one called out because I [Hans] took the crumpled one away from it. Then it stopped calling out, and I sat down on top of the crumpled one.' Freud believed this dream was linked to the boy's experience of entering the parental bed in the mornings – an activity he had greatly enjoyed. However, his father had repeatedly objected, so that Freud interpreted him as the big giraffe protesting at the boy taking the crumpled giraffe (Mrs Graf) away from him. Furthermore, the long neck of the giraffe was interpreted as symbolic of a large phallus.

In short, Hans's phobia of horses was the manifestation of a repressed fear that his father (the horse) would castrate him (by biting) to punish him for the sexual feelings he harboured towards his mother. Freud thus encouraged Graf to reassure his son that he posed no threat to him, and in due course there was a reported alleviation of the symptoms. Two incidents in particular led Freud to believe that Hans was successful in resolving his Oedipus complex. The first was when Graf saw Hans playing with some dolls. Hans told him that he (the boy) was the dolls' father, that his mother was their mother, and Graf their grandfather – an implicit acceptance of his unconscious feelings. The following day Hans imagined a plumber had removed his bottom and 'widdler' only to replace them with new, larger versions – representing a growing confidence in his own sexual place in the world.

The case of Little Hans is one of the most discussed in the history of psychology. For Freud, it was confirmation of years of theoretical thinking and a potent weapon against his opponents. His critics, though, remained unconvinced. There have been consistent doubts about the scientific veracity of the therapy, given that both Freud and the patient's father entered into it sharing common ideas that both were keen to verify. Furthermore, even if Hans's phobia did result from the Oedipus complex, Freud had insufficient evidence to press the universality of the complex as forcefully as he did. As for Hans, he met Freud again when he was nineteen years of age and reported a perfectly normal adolescence. He claimed to have no recollection of the talks with his father that provided the basis of Freud's analysis, and on reading the case notes he said it 'came to him as something unknown'.

Man of Science?

'For I am actually not at all a man of science, not an observer, not an experimenter, not a thinker. I am by temperament nothing but a conquistador – an adventurer if you will – with all the curiosity, daring and tenacity characteristic of a man of this sort.'

SIGMUND FREUD TO WILHELM FLIESS, 1900

The question of the scientific validity of his work dogged Freud in his own lifetime and has continued through to the present day. As we have already seen, Freud yearned to be a great scientist above all else – a thinker in the mould of Copernicus, Darwin, Newton or Einstein. As he expressed it in his own words, shortly before his death in 1938, 'I have spent my whole life standing up for what I have considered to be scientific truth, even when it was uncomfortable and unpleasant for my fellow man.'

On the same theme, he variously referred to psychoanalysis as a 'natural science' and an 'impartial instrument', and described 'the psychoanalytic view' as 'empirical – either a direct expression of observations or the outcome of a process of working them over'. Yet these are difficult assertions to uphold. As early as the 1890s, before he had become a famous name, Freud was provided with a reference from some of his colleagues in Vienna in support of an application he had made for a research post. While acknowledging his undoubted talent, it hinted at the concerns others would more publicly voice in due course as to his scientific methods:

> The novelty of the research, and the difficulty of verifying it, makes it impossible at present to reach a definite judgement as to its importance. It is possible that Freud overestimates it and generalizes too much on the results obtained. At all events his research in this field [psychical research] shows unusual talent and the ability to find new directions for scientific research.

In 1907, his one-time friend and collaborator Josef Breuer warned: 'Freud is a man given to absolute and exclusive formulations; this is a physical need which, in my opinion, leads to excessive generalization.' Carl Jung, meanwhile, would make similar claims about his former mentor prior to and after their split. Another to question his scientific standing was Freud's fellow graduate of the University of Vienna – and arguably the twentieth century's greatest philosopher of science – Karl Popper.

Popper's most important work aimed to establish how any given theory can be tested for its scientific validity. For centuries, the 'scientific method' had involved inductive reasoning – in other words, drawing general conclusions from specific observations. For instance: 'All the swans I have seen are white, therefore all swans are white.' However, as far back as the eighteenth century David Hume had raised problems with the method.

He argued that conclusions drawn in this way were inherently unprovable. For instance, in the case of the swans, you may only say categorically that all swans are white if you have examined every swan ever – clearly an impossibility – and found them to be so. Meanwhile, it takes the appearance of but one black swan to see the theory collapse.

Popper's solution was to approach the question of scientific validity from a completely new angle. In his theory of falsifiability, he argued that a scientific theory is not such because it is proven by experimentation and induction, but because it may be falsifiable (in other words, it has the potential to be disproven by observation). Therefore, the theory that all swans are white could originally have been considered scientific because it could be disproven by observation (such as the observation of a black swan). Furthermore, it could also have been considered true up to the point that it was disproven. In Popper's estimation, however, Freud's work fell short of this scientific threshold. As he put it, Freud and his fellow psychoanalysts 'couched their theories in terms which made them amenable only to confirmation'.

Freud hinted at various points over his life that he recognized the difficulty in establishing the scientific basis of his work. As the quotation at the start of this section suggests, there was a time when Freud felt himself as much on a mission or crusade as on a journey of strictly scientific investigation. He was no doubt buoyed in this by the support he received from Fliess, who in 1895 had assured him:'… we cannot do without men with the courage to think new things before they can prove them'. Indeed, Freud's willingness to get his ideas out there even before he had sufficient empirical evidence to prove them only increased as he grew older. In particular, his diagnosis with cancer in 1923 served to sharpen his desire to publish and be damned.

One of the chief accusations he faced (and continues to face) is that his work was consistently rooted in too little evidence. Time and again, the avant-garde theories that made his name were based on what might be deemed scant anecdotal evidence. Take *Studies on Hysteria* – the work he published with Breuer. It relied on a mere five case studies. Furthermore, as the preface acknowledged, much of the most important testimony was left out for reasons of delicacy:

> Our experience is derived from private practice in an educated and literate social class, and the subject matter with which we deal often touches upon our patients' most intimate lives and histories. It would be a grave breach of confidence to publish material of this kind … It has therefore been impossible for us to make use of some of the most instructive and convincing of our observations. This of course applies especially to all those cases in which sexual and marital relations play an important aetiological part.

Thus it comes about that we are only able to produce very incomplete evidence in favour of our view.

To say, 'Trust us, we have lots of evidence to back this up, only we can't show it to you,' was never going to be sufficient to silence the sceptics.

Yet, no doubt the sensitivity of the subject matter did present real – and sometimes insurmountable – challenges in terms of first finding and then disseminating supporting evidence. As he noted in 1930's *Civilization and Its Discontents*: 'It is not easy to treat feelings scientifically.' Additionally, he was nervous of how the public would react to his patients if he revealed the true extent of his interactions with them. He once spoke of not having 'too much faith in my readers' discretion'. On another occasion he defended his decision to restrict the amount of information he released of his self-analysis, stating, 'The public has no claim to learn any more of my personal affairs.' But if your personal affairs are the basis of your fame and professional standing, the point may be more moot than he gave it credit for. In the introduction to the case study of Dora, he reflected on his previous books and papers: 'No doubt it was awkward that I was obliged to publish the results of my enquiries without there being any possibility of other workers in the field testing and checking them.'

His critics also rounded on his habit of presenting theories that were speculative or fragmentary (and sometimes both) as fully formed. His analysis of dream symbols, for example, could only ever hope to be speculative – for how may one empirically prove that, say, a purse envisaged in a dream is representative of a womb? Nor is it reasonable to believe that, for instance, the Oedipus complex is scientifically verifiable in the way that one might hope to verify the boiling point of water. It is legitimate to question Freud's push to have it accepted as a universal truth. This, we might think, was just the sort of theorizing that drove Popper to distraction. It had a similar effect on the philosopher Ludwig Wittgenstein, who said, 'Freud is constantly claiming to be scientific. But what he gives is speculation – something prior even to the formation of an hypothesis.'

Subsequent scientific investigation has indeed cast grave doubt on many of the key tenets of Freud's vision of psychoanalysis. In the words of Todd Dufresne, a Canadian social and cultural theorist who specializes in Freud: 'Arguably no other notable figure in history was so fantastically wrong about nearly every important thing he had to say.' Few scientists today pay much heed to the Oedipus complex as a genuine driver of human behaviour. Nor is there mainstream acceptance that we are each subject to the interactions of our ego, id and superego, or that we generally follow the fixed pattern of sexual development that Freud laid out. Current understanding of the dream function has also moved far beyond Freud's theses, while his ideas on female sexuality, gender roles and homosexuality are now generally regarded as both erroneous and unhelpful, having been moulded in no small part by the social attitudes of the patriarchal society he inhabited.

And yet … Freud did bring scientific vigour (albeit imperfectly formed) in academic areas where it had been all but absent previously. While great swathes of his ideas have been discredited and debunked, in certain fundamentals he achieved great things. The detail of his model of the unconscious may be scientifically unsupportable, but he brought the role of the unconscious out into the light. His interpretation of dreams is not the full story, but he showed that our dreams can provide us with clues to our underlying mental processes. He may have overestimated the role of the sex drive (and later the death drive), yet few would argue that primal emotional drives are not important to understanding human behaviour. In short, yes, he got things wrong, but not always altogether wrong. And without him, our understanding of the human psyche would likely be light years behind where it is now.

He was, too, admirably open-minded as to where science might lead us. In 'Beyond the Pleasure Principle' (1920), for example, he called biology 'a land of unlimited possibilities … We cannot guess what answers it will return in a few dozen years. They may be of the kind that will blow away the whole of our artificial structure of hypothesis.' So perhaps we may do better to view Freud as other than a scientist in the traditional sense – even though it would doubtless have pained him to have his scientific credentials so undermined. In academic faculties around the world today, you are far more likely to hear Freud mentioned in non-scientific departments. As the erstwhile British writer, psychiatrist and psychoanalyst Anthony Storr put it:

> Very early in its history, psychoanalysis left the narrow confines of the consulting room and made incursions into anthropology, sociology, religion, literature, art and the occult.

Read Like Freud

'Words were originally magic, and to this day words
have retained much of their ancient magical power.
By words one person can make another blissfully
happy or drive him to despair, by words the teacher
conveys his knowledge to his pupils, by words
the orator carries his audience with him and
determines their judgements and decisions.
Words provoke affects and are in general the
means of mutual influence among men.'

SIGMUND FREUD, *INTRODUCTORY LECTURES*, 1917

Freud was a prodigious reader, consuming everything from technical papers and scientific treatises to literary classics from throughout the ages. All texts, without exception, were sources he could use in the development of psychoanalysis, every one of them describing the world (or some aspect of it) as it is perceived in another's mind. While acknowledging that he was profoundly influenced by the writings of myriad scientists, clinicians and fellow psychoanalysts, we shall nonetheless restrict ourselves here to a brief survey of his tastes in more literary fields.

In terms of philosophy, a few names are particularly prominent. He was an avid reader of that giant of the Ancient Greek thinkers, Aristotle, and also admired the British utilitarian John Stuart Mill, some of whose works he translated for publication and whom he once described as 'the man of the century most capable of freeing himself from the domination of the usual prejudices'. Another favourite was Ludwig Feuerbach, whose critique of organized religion in *The Essence of Christianity* was particularly appealing to Freud.

However, it is to Friedrich Nietzsche that Freud is most commonly linked. Indeed, Freud was so acutely aware of being accused of plundering Nietzsche's ideas (Nietzsche lived from 1844 until 1900 and their careers overlapped) that he claimed not to read him. However, his repeated references to Nietzsche suggest otherwise. It is clear he was well aware of much of Nietzsche's output and was a considerable fan, too. He said of Nietzsche that he had a 'more penetrating knowledge of himself than any man who ever lived or was likely to live' and was a 'philosopher whose guesses and intuitions often agree in the most astonishing way with the laborious findings of psychoanalysis'.

Away from philosophy, Freud enjoyed many of the great figures of European literature, not least for the characters they created, upon whom he could test out his ideas. Shakespeare, for example, provided Hamlet, who may be regarded as the archetypal case of an unresolved Oedipus complex. From the ancient world, Freud is known to have read the works of Homer (*The Iliad* and *The Odyssey*) and, of course, Sophocles (author of perhaps the most celebrated narrative of Oedipus). Of a slightly more recent vintage were John Milton (and *Paradise Lost* in particular) and the bounteous works of Goethe (with *Faust*, regarded by some as the single greatest work in the German language, an especial favourite). All these authors richly presented stories that examine the complex interplay between the conscious and unconscious minds, some of them millennia before the concept of the unconscious had even entered into common usage. A highly selective list of other authors that Freud cited over his lifetime includes:

- Eduard Dekker (known by the pseudonym 'Multatuli'). A Dutch writer best known for the satirical novel *Max Havelaar*.
- Charles Dickens – in particular *David Copperfield*, a copy of which Freud gave to Martha on their engagement. He described it as his favourite of Dickens's works because its characters were the most 'individualized' in the Dickens canon and 'sinful without being abominable'.
- Fyodor Dostoyevsky, about whom Freud wrote a famous critical evaluation, which included the description of *The Brothers Karamazov* as '… the most magnificent novel ever written; the episode of the Grand Inquisitor, one of the peaks in the literature of the world, can hardly be valued too highly'.
- Anatole France. French writer whose works include *The White Stone*, which includes a rumination on anti-Semitism and the evolution of the Christian faith.
- Theodor Gomperz. An Austrian philosopher and scholar whose *magnum opus* was *Griechische Denker* (*Greek Thinkers*).
- Heinrich Heine. A German author and poet

whose works Freud drew upon for *Jokes and Their Relation to the Unconscious*.

- Gottfried Keller. Swiss author of *The People of Seldwyla*.
- Rudyard Kipling. The behemoth who straddled English literature from the nineteenth to the twentieth centuries. Freud praised *The Jungle Book*, a collection of fables featuring anthropomorphic animals.
- Lord Macaulay – notably his *Critical and Historical Essays: Contributed to the Edinburgh Review*.
- C. F. Meyer. The Swiss realist poet who authored *Huttens letzte Tage* (*Hutten's Last Days*).
- Dmitry Merezhkovsky. A leading figure in Russia's so-called Silver Age of poetry.
- Mark Twain – especially his artful *Sketches New and Old*.
- Johan Weier (or Weyer). A sixteenth-century Dutch physician. Freud was especially drawn to his writings on witchcraft, and his assertion that some of those accused of sorcery were actually mentally ill (a term it is believed Weier coined).
- Émile Zola. Freud was known to admire *Fécondité*, the first instalment of the *Four Gospels* novel cycle.

While Freud drank deeply from the literary well, he seems, however, to have been less convinced by the output of his own lifetime. In 1908 he commented:

Modern literature is predominantly concerned with the most questionable problems which stir up all the passions, and which encourage sensuality and a craving for pleasure, and contempt for every fundamental ethical principle and every ideal. It brings before the reader's mind pathological figures, and problems concerned with psychopathic sexuality, revolution and other subjects.

Nonetheless, there were one or two of his contemporaries to whom he offered praise. Among them was fellow Austrian, Arthur Schnitzler (1862–1931), best known for 1897's *Reigen*, which caused a scandal at the time for its depiction of ten pairs of characters prior to and following sexual congress. On seeing another of his plays, *Paracelsus*, in 1899, Freud was moved to say he was 'amazed at how much a poet knows'. In 1922, Freud wrote to Schnitzler to tell him that 'you have learned through intuition – though actually as a result of sensitive introspection – everything that I have had to unearth by laborious work on other persons'.

Stefan Zweig (1881–1942) was another Austrian writer who became a personal friend. Though little read today, Zweig was a superstar in the 1920s and 1930s with works such as *The Royal Game, Letter from an Unknown Woman* and *Beware of Pity*. Freud believed Zweig's fiction and non-fiction chimed with many of his own ideas and in 1924 gave Zweig the manuscript of his 1907 lecture

'The Creative Writer and Daydreaming', in which he discussed the notion that creative writing is a form of adult play expressing repressed desires.

A Matter of
Life and Death

'The assumption of the existence of an instinct
of death or destruction has met with
resistance even in analytic circles.'

SIGMUND FREUD, 1930

In 1920, Freud published an essay called 'Beyond the Pleasure Principle'. It turned out to be among the most controversial of his career, with even his most ardent adherents struggling to accept its central thesis: that each human being is subject to an ongoing conflict between their life drive (which he termed Eros) and their death drive (which Freud's sometime acolyte Wilhelm Stekel would come to call Thanatos).

He characterized Eros (from the Ancient Greek for *love*) as responsible for our desire for self-preservation (and preservation of the species) and procreation, along with such positive attributes as creativity, harmony and sexual desire – all channelled via the libido; by contrast he had Thanatos (from the Ancient Greek for *death*) urging us towards ultimate self-destruction and impelling us towards other unhelpful behaviours defined by such negative features as aggression, repetition and compulsion.

This was a great bound away from Freud's earlier model of the self as primarily governed by the pleasure principle – which he said regulated our mental activity towards the goals of producing pleasure and avoiding unpleasure. As the years passed, however, Freud witnessed behaviours in his patients that seemed to go contrary to his assumption that the pleasure principle ruled supreme. In particular:

- He noticed that victims of trauma (and especially those who had endured the horrors of the First World War) would psychologically repeat the index trauma event. For instance, he noted that the dreams of trauma victims often 'have the characteristic of repeatedly bringing the patient back into the situation of his accident'. This clearly did not comply with the pleasure principle since the individual was subconsciously reliving unpleasure.
- He watched his eighteen-month-old grandson repeatedly play a game in which he re-enacted the disappearance of his mother (his mother having left him for a few hours in the normal course of everyday life). 'How then,' Freud pondered, 'does his repetition of this distressing experience as a game fit in with the pleasure principle?'
- He saw patients who had repressed a painful memory reproduce it within their contemporary experience (as neuroses, for instance) rather than placing it within the context of a traumatic event now in the past. He therefore wondered if there was a 'compulsion to repeat' that overrode the pleasure principle.

Freud's striking conclusion was that humans have an urge to 'restore an earlier state of things' – and ultimately to the inorganic state from which all life first emerged. Thus, while Eros drives us towards living, Thanatos yearns for a return to non-life. As he wrote, 'The goal of all life is death, or to express it retrospectively: the inanimate existed before the animate.' While Freud would not have appreciated the biblical allusion, we are put in mind of Genesis 3:19 (King James version): 'In the sweat of thy face shalt thou eat bread, till thou return unto the ground; for out of it wast thou taken: for dust thou art, and unto dust shalt thou return.'

To begin with, even Freud seemed unsure of this dramatic new thesis, writing in his introduction: 'What follows is speculation, often far-fetched speculation, which the reader will consider or dismiss according to his individual predilection.' However, over the next few years he apparently grew in confidence that he was on to something. In 1924, for instance, he proclaimed that the 'libido has the task of making the destroying instinct innocuous, and it fulfils the task by diverting that instinct to a great extent outwards ... The instinct is then called the destructive instinct, the instinct for mastery, or the will to power.' Come 1930 and he wrote the following unequivocal statement in *Civilization and Its Discontents*: 'To begin with it was only tentatively that I put forward the views I have developed here, but in the course of time they have gained such a hold upon me that I can no longer think in any other way.'

Others remained unconvinced, however. The British psychologist William McDougall (1871–1938) described the theory of the death drive as 'the most bizarre monster of all his [Freud's] gallery of monsters'. Even Freud's great cheerleader, Ernest Jones, wrote (as tactfully as possible) in his 1953 biography that 'Beyond the Pleasure Principle' 'displayed a boldness of speculation that was unique in all his writings' and was 'noteworthy in being the only one of Freud's [works] which has received little acceptance on the part of his followers'.

THE AGONY OF EXISTENCE

'The times are gloomy; fortunately it is not my job to brighten them.'

SIGMUND FREUD TO ARNOLD ZWEIG, 1935

The theory of the death drive was in part Freud's solution to a problem that had been troubling him for a long time: if life is ruled by the pleasure principle and driven by the libido, why does so much human behaviour seem directed against inducing pleasure? What, in other words, might be this strange competing drive that works against the desires of the libido? But it seems likely there was more to the formulation of the death drive than just an impartial desire to address a theoretical problem. Freud, by his own admission, was subject to bouts of melancholy and the theory of the death drive was undoubtedly influenced by the depressed view of the world he had around the time he was devising it.

As we have already seen, Freud endured various hardships from childhood into adulthood and he could often appear both gloomy and irascible. However, his view of humanity seems to have taken a new downturn in the face of the First World War and its needless slaughter. For instance, in 1914, the first year of conflict, he wrote to his Russian-born psychoanalysis colleague, Lou Andreas-Salomé: 'I cannot be an optimist, and I believe I differ from the pessimists only insofar as wicked, stupid, senseless things don't upset me, because I have accepted them from the beginning as part of what the world is composed of.' Whether he was really as accepting of those 'wicked, stupid, senseless things' as he claimed is highly doubtful.

In his twin essays collected as 'Reflections on War and Death' in 1915, he retained the sense that life is essentially a burden. 'Bearing life is, after all,' he said, 'the first duty of all living beings.' Two years later, he published another essay, 'Mourning and Melancholia', in which he analysed the differences and similarities between those two states as responses to loss. It was a subject that had acquired a new level of relevance given that a generation of Europe's young men were in the process of being wiped out. In psychological terms, Freud argued that mourning was the conscious (and healthy) process of addressing the grief caused by the loss of a specific beloved object or person, while melancholia is identified as the unconscious grieving for something not fully identified or understood (and is thus deemed pathological, potentially manifesting in somatic symptoms such as insomnia and digestive problems).

The sense that Freud was himself struggling with the weight of the world upon his shoulders is palpable in his writings of this period. Nor did the end of the war bring much respite. The year 1920 was particularly cruel – his beloved daughter Sophie died aged just twenty-six, a victim of the influenza epidemic that swept across Europe in the immediate post-war years. It is notable that he introduced the term 'death drive' to the public just a few weeks after her passing, leaving us to ponder whether life may not have influenced science to some extent.

If 1920 was terrible, 1923 was just as bad. That year, Sophie's four-and-a-half-year-old son Heinz succumbed to tuberculosis – a new and devastating blow as Freud considered him 'the cleverest, sweetest child I have met'. 'I don't think I have ever experienced such grief,' he wrote. 'Fundamentally everything has lost its meaning for me.' In addition, Freud underwent what would be the first of thirty-three agonizing operations after he was diagnosed with cancer of the jaw and palate. In due course, he would have the entire upper jaw and palate on his right side removed, which required him to wear an uncomfortable prosthesis between his mouth and nasal cavity. For the remainder of his life he had problems eating, suffered from deteriorating hearing and was limited in his speech. The cancer – and the attempts at curing it – also left him with virtually non-stop pain, which further contributed to the general sense of melancholy and ennui that punctuated his later life's work.

In 1922 he wrote to Sándor Ferenczi (one of his inner circle) of his 'contempt of people and the detestable world'. At the end of the decade, there was little evidence of a softening in his view as he wrote to Andreas-Salomé: 'In the depths of my heart I can't help being convinced that my dear fellow men, with a few exceptions, are worthless.' But perhaps his disappointment with life is best summed up in his observation to his colleague and confidante Marie Bonaparte, Princess of Denmark and Greece, in 1937: 'The moment one enquires about the sense or value of life one is sick, since objectively neither of them has any existence.'

The Female
of the Species

'The great question that has never been answered
and which I have not yet been able to answer,
despite my thirty years of research into the
feminine soul, is "what does a woman want?"'

SIGMUND FREUD TO MARIE BONAPARTE
(QUOTED BY ERNEST JONES, 1953)

If Freud found his fellow man a mystery and disappointment, it is fair to say that he found women even more mystifying – both on a personal and professional level. Although his entire life may be regarded as an assault on the orthodoxies of society, his attitude to the female gender was significantly influenced by the dominant patriarchal ideologies of his age. Furthermore, so effectively did they penetrate his subconscious that attitudes which the modern reader may perceive as socially constructed he regarded as matters of unassailable fact.

Take, for instance, his explanation for the differing gender expectations within a society: 'Women stand for the interests of the family and sexual life, whereas the work of civilization has become more and more the business of the menfolk, setting them increasingly difficult tasks and obliging them to sublimate their drives – tasks for which women have little aptitude.' Though there is too much in these few brief lines to dissect here, we can immediately recognize Freud's unquestioning imposition of universal values upon the sexes. Women are defined only in terms of the sexual and domestic, while men are forced to suppress their true natures in order to provide. Furthermore, it is clear that Freud believed women incapable of carrying out such 'masculine' work, rather than being merely barred from undertaking it. Unselfconsciously, Freud was simply regurgitating a patriarchal model of society honed over millennia and passing it off as objective truth.

His outlook was no doubt informed by the confusion of personal feelings he had for the many women who played prominent roles in his life, from his mother onwards. Nor was he entirely at home with the concept of love, writing in *Civilization and Its Discontents*: 'We never have so little protection against suffering as when we are in love; we are never so desolate as when we have lost the object of our love or its love for us.' While Freud's career was devoted to creating a better understanding of the human mind, the feelings women induced in him remained persistently beyond his comprehension. In his own words in *The Question of Lay Analysis* (1926): 'We know less about the sexual life of little girls than of boys. But we need not feel ashamed of this distinction; after all, the sexual life of adult women is a "dark continent" for psychology.'

So we come to the curious question of his marriage to Martha Bernays, which endured until the end of his life. Here was a woman he undoubtedly fell in love with – a youthful correspondence with her amounting to some 1,000 letters attests to the fact. The production of six offspring is also indicative. Yet there were consistent hints that all was not as it might appear. Take his comment in

Jokes and Their Relation to the Unconscious in 1905: 'That marriage is not an institution that satisfies the husband's sexuality is something one is not bold enough to say loud and in public ...' To have been a fly on wall at the Freud's breakfast table on the day of publication.

We know that Freud entered upon his adult emotional life conjuring with some unorthodox attitudes to sexual desire and romantic love. In 1912, for example, he wrote:

> It sounds not only disagreeable but also paradoxical, yet it must nevertheless be said that anyone who is to be really free and happy in love must have surmounted his respect for women and have come to terms with the idea of incest with his mother or sister.

It is highly likely that Freud was sexually active before he met Martha but he had never been involved with anyone who inspired such passion in him. However, subsequent to their marriage and the arrival of their children, Martha seems to have assumed a rather asexual role in his life.

That the Freud's marriage soon lost its initial vim and vigour is clearly evident in a pair of statements that may be described as damning with faint praise. In the first, dating from 1912, Freud said of Martha: 'I am thankful to her above all for her many noble qualities, for the children who have turned out so well, and for the fact that she has neither been abnormal nor very often ill.'

MÉNAGE À TROIS?

The matter of Freud's marriage was further complicated by the ongoing presence of Martha's younger and highly desirable sister, Minna. She lived in the Freuds' household from 1895 until 1941 and in some respects became a more constant companion to him than even Martha. Minna was certainly more interested in his work than her elder sister, who was insistent that Freud should demarcate his professional and domestic lives ('psychoanalysis stops at the door of the children's room') and once likened psychoanalysis to pornography in a conversation with a visitor to her house. While Martha kept home, Minna regularly accompanied Freud on his travels, often for extended periods. Jung was one of those who was convinced that Freud and Minna's relationship went beyond what was usual between a brother-in-law and sister-in-law. Indeed, it has been suggested that sometime around 1900 Freud got Minna pregnant and arranged for a termination.

The second comment dates from a conversation he had with Marie Bonaparte in 1936 ahead of his golden wedding anniversary, in which he said of his marriage that it had not been 'a bad solution of the marriage problem'.

Freud's feelings towards, and empathy for, women

may have been influenced by the long-term struggle he waged with his own sexuality, which involved an element of homosexual desire. His attitudes towards homosexuality have been a source of much discussion in the decades following his death. On one hand, he was more broadly sympathetic to homosexuality than many of his contemporaries, as when in 1935 he proclaimed: 'It is a great injustice to persecute homosexuality as a crime, and a cruelty, too.' He also distanced himself from the idea that it was a disease or a sign of moral failing. In a letter to a worried mother who suspected her boy was gay he wrote:

> Homosexuality is assuredly no advantage, but it is nothing to be ashamed of, no vice, no degradation; it cannot be classified as an illness; we consider it to be a variation of the sexual function, produced by a certain arrest of sexual development. Many highly respectable individuals of ancient and modern times have been homosexuals, several of the greatest men among them (Plato, Michelangelo, Leonardo da Vinci, etc).

This was an undoubtedly progressive attitude for the time in certain aspects. He also recognized that homosexuality was far more common than was generally understood, stating in 1908's '"Civilized" Sexual Morality and Modern Nervous Illness':

In addition to all those who are homosexuals by virtue of their organization, or who became so in their childhood, there must be reckoned the great number of those in whom, in their mature years, a blocking of the main stream of their libido has caused a widening in the side-channel of homosexuality.

However, critics point out that Freud ultimately gave mixed messages. He believed that humans are born bisexual (that is to say, capable of sexual feelings towards both sexes) but in general his writings support the notion that homosexuality in adults is a result of unresolved aspects of sexual development. In other words, he viewed homosexuality as abnormal and even perverse. As he went on to tell that worried mother:

In a certain number of cases we succeed in developing the blighted germs of heterosexual tendencies, which are present in every homosexual; in the majority of cases it is no more possible. It is a question of the quality and the age of the individual. The result of treatment cannot be predicted.

Muddying the waters were Freud's own homosexual feelings. The weight of evidence suggests he harboured sexual passion for both Fliess and Jung. Jung acknowledged the 'undeniable erotic undertone' in their relationship while Freud wrote to Fliess to tell him that

'I do not share your contempt for friendship between men' and that 'In my life, as you know, woman has never replaced the comrade, the friend.' By 1910, however, he appears to have felt himself 'cured', writing, in a letter to Ferenczi: 'I feel capable of handling everything and am pleased with the resultant greater independence that comes from having overcome my homosexuality.'

The aggregate result was that Freud's theories regarding women, femininity and homosexuality are far less complete and coherent than his ruminations on the male, heterosexual experience. It may be true to say that while Freud aspired to set out a new framework for understanding the human mind, he was only ever comfortable talking about somewhat less than 50 per cent of the population.

Some, such as feminist writer and activist Kate Millett, consider this rendered him a menace. She descried him, for instance, as 'beyond question the strongest individual counterrevolutionary force in the ideology of sexual politics' who enabled men to 'rationalize the invidious relationship between the sexes, to ratify traditional roles'. Others, however, have been more sympathetic, such as the academic and social commentator Camille Paglia, who in 1991 wrote: 'Trying to build a sex theory without studying Freud, women have made nothing but mud pies.'

Watch Your Tongue

'I am very often faced with the task of discovering, from the patient's apparently casual utterances and associations, a thought-content which is at pains to remain concealed but which cannot nevertheless avoid unintentionally betraying its existence in a whole variety of ways. Slips of the tongue often perform a most valuable service here ...'

SIGMUND FREUD, *THE PSYCHOPATHOLOGY OF EVERYDAY LIFE*, 1901

In the volume quoted above, Freud introduced the idea of parapraxis – that an apparent error in speech, memory or action is not an error at all but rather a reflection of unconscious mental processes. The world embraced the idea most enthusiastically in the form of the 'slip of the tongue' (also known as the Freudian slip).

For instance, Freud cited an occasion when the president of Austria's lower house opened what he knew would be a hostile session by 'herewith declaring the sitting closed'. Freud argued that he said 'closed' (rather than 'opened') not simply because he accidentally stumbled upon the wrong word but because he was voicing an unconscious wish (that the session be over) – in other words, parapraxes are 'not chance events but serious mental acts; they have a sense; they arise from concurrent action – or perhaps rather, the mutually opposing action – of two different intentions'.

Yet a parapraxis need not necessarily be a slip of the tongue. It might just as easily be a misreading or

Freud noted that parapraxis can occur in three different forms:
- Where the subject is aware of the rival 'disturbing' intention but does not recognize it before he makes the slip
- Where the subject is aware of the rival 'disturbing' intention and recognizes it even before he makes the slip
- Where the subject refuses to acknowledge the rival 'disturbing' intention either before or after the slip

In each case, 'the suppression of the speaker's intention to say something is the indispensable condition of the occurrence of a slip of the tongue'.

mishearing, a slip of the pen (or keyboard), an incidence of temporary forgetting or even the mislaying of an object – any action, in other words, that might be interpreted as symptomatic of a hidden motive. Freud actually used the German word *Fehlleistungen*, which has the meaning of *faulty actions*. *Parapraxes*, a Greek word, was the choice of one of his English translators. So, for instance, Freud recounted an episode in which he repeatedly forgot to buy some blotting paper. In German, blotting paper may be translated as either *Löschpapier* or, more pertinently, *Fliesspapier*. At the time of this incidence of temporary amnesia, Freud's once firm friendship with Wilhelm Fliess was coming under strain. Freud retrospectively interpreted his forgetfulness as reflecting his desire to forget all things to do with Fliess, including *Fliesspapier*.

Probably the most famous of the 'faulty actions' he analysed is that known as the Signorelli parapraxis. On his travels, Freud had marvelled at the Last Supper frescoes painted by Luca Signorelli in a church in the Italian city of Orvieto. However, when he later tried to recall the name of the artist, he was unable to do so. Instead he came up with the names of two alternative artists – Botticelli and Boltraffio. Freud gave a detailed explication of how he came to link the names of these three artists.

The *Bo* of Botticelli he linked with Bosnia, which had been the subject of a conversation he had been conducting with a stranger on a train shortly before his failure to remember Signorelli's name. Furthermore, he connected Signorelli's name with the Spanish *Signor* (Sir) and its German equivalent, *Herr*, which in turn he related to Herzegovina. The precise subject of his on-train discussion was the habits of the Turks in Bosnia-Herzegovina. This led Freud to consider anecdotal evidence that the Turks were prone to allow sexual disturbances to drive them to despair. In regard to Boltraffio, meanwhile, he forged a linguistic connection with the Italian city of Trafoi, where he had recently received news that one of his patients suffering from sexual problems had killed themselves.

It was this distressing memory that Freud concluded he was really trying to suppress, but which manifested as forgetting Signorelli's name. The substitute names his memory retrieved nonetheless revealed the true nature of his motive to forget, since the names of Botticelli and Boltraffio subconsciously put him in mind of the themes of sex and death, and by extension the sad fate of his patient.

The Signorelli parapraxis has received innumerable secondary interpretations over the years and Freud's version has been strongly criticized for a lack of linguistic vigour and the failure to consider the content of the frescoes themselves in relation to the act of forgetting. Nonetheless, it stands as the first and most famous parapraxis that Freud ever produced. It was a phenomenon, too, that he was unwilling to underestimate, as when he wrote, 'I am not asserting ... that every single parapraxis that occurs has a sense, even though I regard that as probably the case.'

When is a Joke Not a Joke?

'A physician, leaving a woman's sickbed, shakes his head and says to her husband accompanying him: "I don't like the look of your wife." "I haven't liked the look of her for a long time," the husband hastens to agree.'

SIGMUND FREUD, *JOKES AND THEIR RELATION TO THE UNCONSCIOUS* (1905)

It is often said that if you have to explain a joke, it's probably not a very funny one. Similarly, any joke will likely lose its comic impact in the face of excessive analysis. Yet from a psychologist's point of view, Freud thankfully did not concern himself with such matters. He was quite happy to analyse jokes to the point that all the humour was drained from them. In his own words, 'When we are laughing really heartily at a joke, we are not exactly in the most suitable state of mind to inquire into its techniques.'

By minutely deconstructing jokes and their contents, he sought to prove his belief that they offer piercing insights into our unconscious thoughts. In *Jokes and Their Relation to the Unconscious*, Freud differentiated dreams and jokes thus: 'The dream predominantly serves to spare ourselves unpleasure, the joke to gain pleasure; but in these two aims, all our psychical activities meet.' He argued that jokes serve as a window not only into the usually hidden thoughts of the joke-teller but of their audience as well, and even society in general. Freud enjoyed the linguistic mechanics of joke-telling and was a notoriously big fan of the pun. But mostly he was fascinated by what a joke attempts to hide and what it inadvertently reveals. In jest there is truth, he suggested, just as it is present in a Freudian slip. In his analysis, Freud was greatly influenced by the German philosopher Theodor Lipps, who in 1898 published *Komik und Humor*. In that work he asserted that to understand how jokes work, we should look not to 'the contents of the conscious' but instead focus on 'inherently unconscious mental processes'.

For Freud, joke-telling is a means to satisfy a primitive aggressive drive in humans. By their nature, jokes subvert typical mechanisms of repression and suppression. They allow us to frame ideas and feelings that might otherwise be left unexplored. In that sense, the audience is as involved in the subversion as the teller. Indeed, the very act of laughing may be seen as a physical manifestation of denied inhibition. And Freud being Freud, he was primarily interested in what jokes tell us about the sexual unconscious of the joker and the audience by permitting the collective breaking of sexual taboos (in verbal form, at least).

He also recognized that jests commonly negate other cultural inhibitions. Jokes, after all, may variously allow you to attack an enemy, an underdog or an outsider, and to ridicule authority. In *Jokes and Their Relation to the Unconscious*, he wrote, 'Where a joke is not an end in itself, i.e. innocuous, it puts itself at the service of two tendencies only, which can themselves be merged into a single viewpoint; it is either a *hostile* joke (used for aggression, satire, defence) or an *obscene* joke (used to strip someone naked).' Even the 'innocuous joke' has deeper motives, such as 'the ambiguous urge to show off how clever one is, to display oneself, a drive to be equated with exhibitionism in the field of sexuality'.

While Freud's writings on jokes are notable for their lack of laughs and a determinedly serious tone, his dry analyses make many important points that hold true today as much as they did when he was composing his papers. For instance, as a Jew living in an era of increasing anti-Semitism, he wrote, 'The jokes made about Jews by outsiders are mostly brutal comic anecdotes, in which the effort of making a proper joke is saved by the fact that to the outsider the Jew counts as a comical figure.' Over a century later, there are still plentiful 'comedians' who mine a seam of comedy rooted in subconscious racist and xenophobic stereotypes.

Meanwhile, another analysis in *Jokes and Their Relation to the Unconscious* provides an insight into how Freud could take a quip and mine it for evidence of its subconscious sexual origins (as well as, perhaps subconsciously, to hint at circumstances within his own marriage). The original gag goes like this: 'A wife is like an umbrella … sooner or later one takes a cab.' (*Cab* in early twentieth-century Vienna was slang for a prostitute.) Freud explained:

The simile may be worked out as follows. One marries in order to protect oneself against the temptations of sensuality, but it turns out nevertheless that marriage does not allow of the satisfaction of needs that are somewhat stronger than usual. In just the same way, one takes an umbrella with one to protect oneself from the rain and nevertheless gets wet in the rain. In both cases one must look around for a stronger protection: in the latter case one must take a public vehicle, and in the former a woman who is accessible in return for money ... One does not venture to declare aloud and openly that marriage is not an arrangement calculated to satisfy a man's sexuality unless one is driven to do so perhaps by a love of truth ... The strength of this joke lies in the fact that nevertheless – in all kinds of roundabout ways – it has declared it.

So it is that we get an answer to the question, 'When is a joke not a joke?' Today, Freud's studies on jokes are less celebrated than his work on, say, the interpretation of dreams or the development of infantile sexuality. Yet, dense read as they may be, they played an important role within the context of his wider intellectual output, serving to fulfil his aim of expanding psychoanalysis into 'spheres of universal interest'.

Society Against the Self

'Generally speaking, our civilization is built up
on the suppression of the instincts.'

SIGMUND FREUD, '"CIVILIZED" SEXUAL MORALITY
AND MODERN NERVOUS ILLNESS', 1908

Freud was always interested in exploring how his ideas relating to the psyche of the individual might be extended to society in general. It was an area of study towards which he devoted a considerable amount of time in the latter decades of his career. Much of what he argued was also highly divisive, prompting vehement attacks from his critics and forcing even some of his most keen followers to distance themselves from his conclusions.

His methodology to this end might be broadly characterized as a process of analysing social interactions, rituals and other modes of behaviour to determine the repressed motivations behind them. In 1939, Freud wrote *Moses and Monotheism*, a book questioning key parts in the given life of the biblical figure of Moses. Freud's analysis was regarded by some as innovative and insightful and by others as historical bunkum. In terms of his general approach, the comments of the philosopher Mikkel Borch-Jacobsen and psychologist Sonu Shamdasani are instructive. They argued that Freud examined societies using 'the same method of interpretation that he used in the privacy of his office to "reconstruct" his patients' forgotten and repressed memories'.

Probably the high point of his 'psychoanalysis' of society was 1930's *Civilization and Its Discontents*. Its underlying argument is that all society is beset by tension between the desires of the individual and the demands of society; or to put it another way, there is a fundamental clash between nature and civility. In Freud's own words: 'The replacement of the power of the individual by that of the community is the decisive step towards civilization.'

But if society works contrary to the drives of the individual, how did society ever come to exist? After all, human beings are, as he noted in 1905, 'tireless pleasure-seekers', but society – in its imposition of duties and responsibilities – regularly mitigates against the achievement of pleasure. The reason, he posits, is the desire for security. Man's libidinal urges and resulting propensity for aggression towards whatever stands in his way are ultimately harmful if left unfettered. We might literally kill each other in pursuit of gratification. So society came together to outlaw, *inter alia*, murder, rape and adultery. As he put it, 'Civilization therefore obtains mastery over the individual's dangerous desire for aggression by weakening and disarming it and by setting up an agency within him to watch over it, like a garrison in a conquered city.' Furthermore, many of those tasks necessary to provide the staples of human life are more efficiently carried out within cooperative groups. Therefore, 'Civilized man has traded in a portion of his chances of happiness for a certain measure of security.'

Yet, according to Freud, this social contract brings new sources of hostility as the individual reins in their natural drives to conform to society's demands. Women sacrifice their own pleasure for the good of their children, while men channel a proportion of their libidinal energies into works that serve the needs of the wider society. Women, furthermore, harbour resentment at society for their exclusion from non-domestic work. As society seeks to bring its population to ever more peaceful coexistence, so the needs of the many are privileged over those of the individual, leading to increasing discontent.

Freud then went on to explore how religion may be used as a coping strategy for those desirous of building a wall between themselves and the general suffering evident in society. Yet, he continued, even as religion cultivates society by taming primal instincts and encouraging a shared belief system, it unleashes psychological warfare upon the individual who must subjugate themselves not only to society but to the godhead too.

He also pondered the extent to which we have natural instincts in opposition to those of the pleasure-seeking libido, giving rise to his description of the death instinct (as detailed on page 123). This in turn raised the prospect that humanity is ultimately a destructive force, and that society strives to repress our natural aggression.

Redirected back towards ourselves, aggression manifests as the superego, burdening us with regret for the wrongs we commit and guilt even for those we have only thought about. Guilt, and associated discontent, thus becomes a pre-requisite of good citizenship. Freud also posited the idea of a cultural superego – a sort of over-arching conscience for the whole of society that imposes yet more regulation on the individual, so fostering still further dissatisfaction.

It is, all in all, a pretty bleak picture of society – an institution in which we are compelled to conform at the expense of our own true wishes. Indeed, he saw society as one of the three prime causes of human suffering:

> We are threatened with suffering from three directions: from our own body, which is doomed to decay and dissolution and which cannot even do without pain and anxiety as warning signals; from the external world, which may rage against us with overwhelming and merciless forces of destruction; and finally from our relations to other men. The suffering which comes from this last source is perhaps more painful than any other.

Nor did he hold out much hope that we have facility to improve the situation greatly, given our tendency towards glib acceptance of socially imposed norms:

It is impossible to escape the impression that people commonly use false standards of measurement – that they seek power, success and wealth for themselves and admire them in others, and that they underestimate what is of true value in life.

Freud on War

'As long as the conditions of life of the various nations are so different and the conflicts between them so violent, wars will be inevitable.'

SIGMUND FREUD, 'REFLECTIONS ON WAR AND DEATH', 1915

Freud's analysis of society was the result of years of thought and went far beyond a knee-jerk reaction to contemporary socio-economic realities. That said, it is worth noting the peculiar cocktail of circumstances – personal and otherwise – in which Freud found himself as he composed his most important works on the psyche of society.

As the 1920s progressed he was getting old, suffered terrible ill health (including debilitating cancer) and had been overcome by personal tragedy too, losing a daughter and grandchild in quick succession. But perhaps most importantly, he had been deeply impacted by the dreadful events of the First World War and the economic and social turmoil that followed it (Freud personally lost a fortune in the post-war economic collapse). Furthermore, by the end of the 1920s it was clear that extremist politics were on the rise in Europe, hand-in-hand with a surge of anti-Semitic feeling. Nor did he have much faith that Marxism was equipped to address the emergence of fascism, having come to believe that in its lack of self-criticism and its promise of a better life for its believers, it echoed many of the problems he saw in organized religion. Consider this scathing assessment of communism in *Civilization and Its Discontents*:

> The communists think they have found the way to redeem mankind from evil. Man is unequivocally good and well disposed to his neighbour, but his nature has been corrupted by the institution of private property. Ownership of property gives the individual the power, and so the temptation, to mistreat his neighbour; whoever is excluded from ownership is bound to be hostile to the oppressor and rebel against him. When private property is abolished, when goods are held in common and enjoyed by all, ill will and enmity among human beings will cease. Because all needs will be satisfied, no one will have any reason to see another person as his enemy; everyone will be glad to undertake whatever work is necessary. I am not concerned with economic criticisms of the communist system; I have no way of knowing whether the abolition of private property is expedient and beneficial. But I can recognize the psychological presumption behind it as a baseless illusion.

Freud had initially been a supporter of the Austro-German alliance as it embarked upon the First World War but it did not take long for him to realize the folly of the entire enterprise. As the dead piled up on the Eastern and Western Fronts, he came to see the conflict as a horrible expression of man's innate aggression (both as individuals and within wider social groups) – a characteristic he described as 'the greatest impediment to civilization'. Even as the individual curbs their personal aggression in line with social expectations, so Freud noted the historical habit of groups channelling their collective aggression outwards towards rival groups. 'One need not be a sentimentalist,' he wrote, 'one may realize the biological and physiological necessity of suffering in the economy of human life, and yet one may condemn the methods and the aims of war and long for its termination.'

As he wrote in a letter of 1918: 'I do not break my head very much about good and evil, but I have found little that is "good" about human beings on the whole.' He simply did not believe that the human species is inclined towards behaving in consistently moral and peaceful ways, given what he once described as our 'primitive, savage and evil impulses'.

An extraordinary correspondence between Freud and Albert Einstein, published in 1933 as *Why War?*, is especially useful in gauging Freud's views on war in his later years. He began the correspondence with the following observation:

Today we see law and violence as opposites. It is easy to demonstrate that the one has developed out of the other, and if we return to the very beginnings and check how it was that this first occurred, the solution of the problem presents itself to us without any difficulties … Conflicts of interest between human beings are in principle resolved by the use of violence. That is how things are throughout the whole of the animal kingdom, from which man should not exclude himself.

Freud was not, it should be said, without theoretical hope. He suggested, for instance, that ever-larger communities of common interest offered the prospect of enduring peace. In practical terms, he recommended the establishment of a central organization established by consensus to deal with international conflicts of interest – an organization that could serve as a peacekeeper, and one with more teeth than the extant League of Nations. Nonetheless, he saw little realistic chance of it happening:

It is all too clear that the nationalistic ideas, paramount today in every country, operate in quite a contrary direction. Some there are who hold that the Bolshevist conceptions may make an end of war, but, as things are, that goal lies very far away and, perhaps, could only be attained after a spell of brutal internecine warfare. Thus it would seem that any effort to replace brute force by the might of an ideal is, under present conditions, doomed to fail.

However, he did wonder whether cultural development might offer the greatest long-term chance of peace. 'On the psychological side,' he observed, 'two of the most important phenomena of culture are, firstly, a strengthening of the intellect, which tends to master our instinctive life, and, secondly, an introversion of the aggressive impulse, with all its consequent benefits and perils.' But again, his scepticism as to its chances of success were clear:

> How long have we to wait before the rest of men turn pacifist? Impossible to say, and yet perhaps our hope that these two factors – man's cultural disposition and a well-founded dread of the form that future wars will take – may serve to put an end to war in the near future, is not chimerical. But by what ways or byways this will come about, we cannot guess. Meanwhile we may rest on the assurance that whatever makes for cultural development is working also against war.

Ultimately, war – and especially modern warfare in all its ruthless efficiency – appalled Freud, but he saw little in the psyche and organization of society to suggest it would, or even could, be consigned to history. But mankind's willingness to expose itself to the pitiless suffering inherent in war still astounded him in its irrationality:

Every man has a right over his own life and war destroys lives that were full of promise; it forces the individual into situations that shame his manhood, obliging him to murder fellow men, against his will; it ravages material amenities, the fruits of human toil, and much besides. Moreover, wars, as now conducted, afford no scope for acts of heroism according to the old ideals and, given the high perfection of modern arms, war today would mean the sheer extermination of one of the combatants, if not of both. This is so true, so obvious, that we can but wonder why the conduct of war is not banned by general consent.

Yet not even Freud could envisage the new levels of savagery to which the world would subject itself, barely twenty years after the First World War was brought to an end. Just a year after his postal conversation with Einstein, Freud's books were burned at Nazi rallies amid the call: 'Against the soul-destroying glorification of the instinctual life, for the nobility of the human soul!' Freud suggested civilization had come some way, at least – Hitler was overseeing the conflagration of the books of Jews, he said, whereas in previous generations it would have been the authors themselves who burned. The Holocaust was but nine years away.

Build a Movement

'A man must get himself talked about.'

SIGMUND FREUD TO MARTHA BERNAYS, 1884

Freud was imbued with ambition from a young age but it was only in his more mature years that he was able to build up the network he needed to truly achieve his goals. The most important of these was to progress psychoanalysis on the international stage, which in turn would bring him the financial security and personal acclaim he yearned for.

While Freud had always inhabited a place outside of mainstream society, he recognized that in order to fulfil his ambitions he could not go it alone but must call upon the help of others. He had been adept at building useful alliances since infancy, for instance forging a close friendship with his nephew John (the son of one of Jacob Freud's children from his first marriage and actually slightly older than Sigmund). Then there were the bonds formed at school with a series of bright boys who did not judge him for being Jewish and who enjoyed his taste for intellectual discussion. He continued to bridge-build in the early part of his career, even as his increasingly radical ideas struggled to get a popular foothold – allying himself first with Josef Breuer and later Wilhelm Fliess when no one else showed much interest in his work.

By the turn of the century, his star was on the rise and he was beginning to leverage greater influence. The need to capitalize on his growing status was never more acute. He was by then a married father of six who also had elderly parents to support. In 1898, he told Fliess that '… wealth brings so little happiness. Money was not a childhood wish.' It might not have bought him happiness, but it is clear that he hungered for the peace of mind that comes with it. As late as 1930, he was still bemoaning his comparative lack of an economic safety net, telling Stefan Zweig, 'How often do I not envy Einstein the youth and energy which enable him to support so many causes with such vigour. I am not only old, feeble and tired, but I am also burdened with heavy financial obligations.'

Under these domestic pressures, Freud developed into a wily strategist as he sought to position the psychoanalytic movement in the early years of the twentieth century. Believing psychoanalysis contained within it the potential to change mankind for the better, he was determined to build a movement around it. His efforts began in earnest in 1902, shortly after he had secured an assistant professorship at the University of Vienna. On the back of publication of *The Interpretation of Dreams* and *The Psychopathology of Everyday Life*, he started to host a discussion group at his home each

Wednesday evening (the group would soon become known as the Wednesday Psychological Society). He viewed it as a forum where he could introduce his ideas to an audience of bright young minds chosen by his own hand. Each session would begin with Martha serving the assembled gathering black coffee and cigars, whereupon Freud would make his entrance. He then customarily delivered a talk on his latest ideas – usually delivered, it was reported, with unstinting self-confidence – while his audience took down notes and prepared their critiques.

While debate was a crucial element of these meetings, Freud nonetheless emerged as a figure of leadership. Indeed, the members appeared to some observers more like apostles gathered round a messiah. As one of the earliest members, Wilhelm Stekel, put it: '… we were like pioneers in a newly discovered land, and Freud was the leader. A spark seemed to jump from one mind to the other, and every evening was like a revelation.'

Freud now had a strong base from which to promote his work, and he had no intention of resting on his laurels. In 1908 the Wednesday Psychological Society was reconstituted as the more grandly named Vienna Psychoanalytic Society, which duly held its first International Congress in Salzburg. With Freud keen to extend his influence beyond Vienna, a Berlin Psychoanalytic Society was also established.

By 1909 momentum was building. The *Yearbook of Psychosomatic and Psychopathological Investigations* (known

> **ALL WELCOME**
>
> Freud was aware of the heavy Jewish bias among his adherents. While he appreciated the spirit of intellectual investigation he considered a feature of European Jewry, he was nervous that unless the organization's ranks were expanded with non-Jews, the movement itself would stall. He was thus delighted when a Swiss gentile psychiatrist called Eugen Bleuler made contact around 1904 and subsequently introduced a young colleague of his, Carl Jung, into proceedings. So began the complex interplay between the two greatest figures of twentieth-century psychotherapy.

as the *Jahrbuch*) appeared for the first time and served as a showcase for the latest ideas in psychoanalysis. Furthermore, Freud (accompanied by fellow members Jung and Sándor Ferenczi) undertook an extremely successful trip to the USA – even if Freud did not much enjoy his stay there. He realized that things were progressing nicely when he saw a member of the crew aboard the ship that took him across the Atlantic reading one of his books. The following year, the International Psychoanalytical Association (IPA) came into being, with Jung as its first president.

Build a Movement

Freud had succeeded in taking psychoanalysis and cultivating it into an international movement. It was an extraordinary achievement, even if cracks in its fabric would soon emerge. Whether it made him happy to secure the wealth and fame he had hungered after for so long is, however, far from clear. As he told fellow psychoanalyst Max Eitingon in 1922: 'I am relieved of material worries, surrounded by popularity which is distasteful to me, and involved in enterprises which rob me of the time and leisure for calm scientific work.'

Below is a roll call of some of the most influential figures in the psychoanalytic movement's early days:

- Karl Abraham (1877–1925; German). A talented medical student, Abraham took up a post in a Swiss psychiatric hospital where he worked alongside Eugen Bleuler and Carl Jung, who introduced him to Freud's work. He first encountered Freud personally in 1907 and soon became not only a professional collaborator but a friend too – Freud would in due course call him his 'best pupil'. Particularly associated with evolving Freud's theories of psychosexual development. He was among the first to warn Freud of the threat posed by Carl Jung (see page 178) to certain Freudian orthodoxies. In 1910 Abraham moved to Berlin to help establish the psychoanalytic society there, which survived his premature death from cancer only to be snuffed out by the rise of

Nazism. He was also president of the IPA from 1914 to 1918 and again in 1925.

- Alfred Adler (1870–1937; Austrian). A Viennese-based doctor and one of Freud's earliest followers, taking part in the inaugural meetings of the Wednesday Psychological Society. However, his relationship with Freud quickly strained. Ambitious in his own right, he questioned the completeness of such fundamental ideas as the Oedipus complex. He was disgruntled when Jung was appointed president of the International Psychoanalytical Association in 1910 – a position he believed should have been his. Already co-editor of the association's monthly journal, *Zentralblatt für Psychoanalyse* (*Central Review of Psychoanalysis*), he refused Freud's offer of the leadership of the Vienna Psychoanalytic Society. He broke with Freud in 1911 to establish what would become the Society for Individual Psychology, taking nine of Freud's Viennese contingent with him.

- Max Eitingon (1881–1943; Russian). Having moved to Germany at the age of twelve, Eitingon read medicine in Zurich and was among those early Freud followers who worked first with Bleuler and Jung. He subjected himself to analysis by Freud in 1908 and subsequently became a practitioner himself. He based himself in Berlin and was invited by Freud to join the Secret Committee aimed at protecting Freud's vision for the movement amid the internal disputes that overtook the group in the 1910s. Hailing from a wealthy family and blessed with great organizational skills, Eitingon was a vital cog in the machine that supported the growth of international psychoanalysis. Financially ruined when Nazism took hold in Germany and existentially threatened as a Jew, he moved to Palestine, where he established another branch of the movement. After Abraham's death, it was he who took over the leadership of the IPA. Posthumously, he has been accused of being part of a Soviet assassination ring, although the charges have never been conclusively proved.

- Sándor Ferenczi (1873–1933; Hungarian). Having graduated in medicine in Vienna, Ferenczi was already established as a neurologist and psychiatrist before joining forces with Freud in 1908. He was renowned for his sensitive treatment of patients and was thus presented with many of the most challenging cases that came before the group. He was president of the IPA from 1918 to 1919. However, by the 1920s he was diverging from Freud in several important respects – not least in advocating more direct interventions in treatment than Freud espoused.

- Ernest Jones (1879–1958; British). Born in Wales, Jones qualified as a doctor specializing in neurology. Increasingly interested in the treatment of the mentally ill, he first encountered Freud's work around 1903 and sought to use many of its ideas in his own practice. He met Jung in Switzerland in 1907, and Freud at the first congress on psychoanalysis in Salzburg a year later. Jones spent the next four years working in Canada before returning to Britain. By now he was the leading English-speaking exponent of psychoanalysis in the world. In 1913 he founded the London Psychoanalytic Society, setting up the British Psychoanalytical Society six years later. He would duly report to Freud that psychoanalysis in Britain 'stands in the forefront of medical, literary and psychological interest'. He was notably loyal to Freud over many years, even though Freud had effectively vetoed Jones's earlier hopes of a romance with his daughter, Anna, who in due course would carve out an illustrious career of her own in psychoanalysis. He served two spells as president of the International Psychoanalytical Association (1920–24 and 1932–49) and was also instrumental in getting Freud out of Vienna and safely established in London in 1938. Jones saw himself as a guardian of Freud's work and devoted his life to spreading the gospel of psychoanalysis. He was also responsible for one of the most important biographies by a contemporary of the man himself.

• Carl Jung (1875–1961; Swiss). Jung made his name working with Eugen Bleuler at Zurich's psychiatric hospital. He first met Freud in 1907 and the two immediately hit it off. Not least, Freud saw an opportunity to improve the international standing of his movement via Jung and Bleuler, who were notable among early adherents for being neither Austrian nor Jewish. Indeed, Freud came to regard Jung as a sort of son and heir within the movement although, as we shall see, their story was not to have a happy ending.

• Otto Rank (1884–1939; Austrian). Rank was something of an intellectual prodigy. In 1905, when he was just twenty-one years old, he approached Freud with an essay (on the subject of 'the artist') that so impressed Freud that he invited the youngster to become secretary of the nascent Vienna Psychoanalytic Society. He also encouraged Rank in his studies, which culminated in him receiving his PhD in 1911 for what may be considered the first Freudian doctoral thesis. He was a prodigious author of psychoanalytic papers, second only to Freud himself. In fact, he was seen by many as his mentor's right-hand man, especially after relations with Jung soured. He was particularly effective in applying psychoanalytic theory to legend, myth and cultural production. Secretary of the International Psychoanalytical Association from 1915 until 1918, he was inducted into Freud's Secret Committee. He worked closely with Ferenczi in the 1920s towards a more proactive therapeutic practice, even in the face of Freud's admonitions. In 1924 he published a paper that questioned the validity of the Oedipus complex – the first time a Freud adherent had publicly voiced doubts. The incident left Freud 'boiling with rage'. In 1926 Rank left for Paris and spent the remainder of his life working there and in New York.

- Hanns Sachs (1881–1947; Austrian). A lawyer by profession, he was notable as the first non-medic to be accepted by Freud into his psychoanalytic inner circle, joining the group's weekly meetings around 1910. He proved a loyal ally, particularly in the period when Freud was experiencing troubles with Adler and Stekel. In 1912 he joined Freud's Secret Committee. In the same year, he and Otto Rank began to edit the *Imago* magazine, which focused on non-clinical applications of psychoanalysis. Prone to ill health, Sachs relocated to Berlin to teach. Fearing rule under Hitler, he emigrated to Boston, USA, in 1932. As Freud faced death, he is said to have told Sachs: 'I know I have at least one friend in America.'

- Wilhelm Stekel (1868–1940; Austrian). Born in what is now part of Ukraine, Stekel first encountered Freud in 1902 when he requested an analysis. He soon joined Freud's Wednesday evening group and struck up a particularly close friendship with Adler. The two oversaw the movement's monthly journal, *Zentralblatt für Psychoanalyse*, but Freud grew vexed by various positions they took contrary to his own. Stekel eventually resigned from the Vienna Psychoanalytic Society but Ernest Jones would say of him: 'Stekel may be accorded the honour, together with Freud, of having founded the first psychoanalytic society.' He committed suicide in 1940.

Our Friend, the Enemy

'My emotional life has always insisted that I should have an intimate friend and a hated enemy.'

SIGMUND FREUD, *THE INTERPRETATION OF DREAMS*, 1899

Despite his formidable success in building an army of supporters, Freud's life was also notable for a series of relationship breakdowns. It was a trend that began early – for example, his childhood friendship with his nephew, John, was subject to a series of fallings-out. As he noted in *The Interpretation of Dreams*: 'We had loved each other and fought with each other; and this childhood relationship ... had a determining influence on all my subsequent relations with contemporaries ...'

So the record proves. The highly fruitful relationship with Breuer was unable to survive the relative lack of success of their *Studies on Hysteria* and Freud's increasing insistence on the sexual underpinnings of the psyche. Then came the even more devastating fall out with Fliess, who propped up Freud for several years when he seemed destined to be nothing more than a voice in the wilderness. After years of extraordinarily intimate correspondence, in which they shared personal and professional secrets, they met in person for the last time in 1900 and sent their final letters in 1902 as disagreements strained the friendship. Fliess had also become convinced that Freud was sharing Fliess's work with third parties – claims Freud fiercely refuted. After some Freud associates issued a paper that Fliess believed plundered his own theses, in 1906 he published some letters from Freud in a bid to prove his case. Freud was appalled by the episode and in response set fire to many of his own papers the following year in what has been seen as an attempt to prevent further breaches of his privacy.

Bitter disputes became a hallmark of the various Psychoanalytic Societies – as a glance at the pen-portraits of its early members hint at. The first serious collapse in relations was with Alfred Adler in 1911. As the founder of psychoanalysis, Freud considered it his exclusive right to define what the movement stood for and he struggled to broach dissent. The vitriol he felt towards Adler was apparent in the note in his 1914 work, *On the History of the Psychoanalytic Movement* – itself an attempt to wrestle control of the narrative of the movement's past and future: 'Everything Adler has to say about dreams, the shibboleth of psychoanalysis, is equally empty and unmeaning.' (Freud had a feel for ruthless put-downs, such as his observation about German psychologist Albert Moll: 'He had stunk up the room like the devil himself, and partly for lack of conviction and partly because he was my guest, I hadn't lambasted him enough.')

After the fall out with Adler came a painful dispute with

Stekel, and many more would follow. By far the one that most upset Freud was the breakdown of his relationship with Jung. Around 1913, Ernest Jones approached Freud with the idea of setting up an inner-inner-circle (which became known as the Secret Committee) with a remit to head-off other disputes and generally protect the good name and the future of the movement.

Freud readily agreed and initially appointed Jones, Karl Abraham, Sándor Ferenczi, Otto Rank and Hanns Sachs. Max Eitingon was added in 1919. For a decade or so it efficiently carried out its role, even in the face of the First World War, which presented significant practical difficulties to the running of the IPA. However, around 1924 dissension from Rank and Ferenczi saw the Secret Committee dissolved and reconstituted. Freud's daughter Anna was brought in to ensure her father's interests were strongly represented – an important staging post in the career of Anna, who did much to preserve and extend her father's legacy as well as to pioneer new psychoanalytic approaches of her own until her death in 1982.

The emergence of any international movement (particularly one that is intellectual in nature) is bound to have its testing episodes. Yet Freud was drawn into confrontations with extraordinary frequency. While he longed to share his ideas with the world, his expectation that those ideas should remain under his control made the locking of horns an inevitable – if exhausting – feature of his life.

FREUD VS JUNG

> 'Jung is crazy, but I really don't want a split; I should
> prefer him to leave of his own accord.'
>
> **SIGMUND FREUD TO KARL ABRAHAM, 1913**

What made the split with Jung so much worse than the others was the high hopes Freud had invested in the Swiss. Their relationship was intense from the outset. Shortly after they met in 1907, Jung wrote to Freud:

> ...my veneration for you has something of the character of a 'religious crush'. Though it does not really bother me, I still feel it is disgusting and ridiculous because of its undeniable erotic undertone. This abominable feeling comes from the fact that as a boy I was the victim of a sexual assault by a man I once worshipped.

By 1909 Freud saw Jung – this well respected non-Jew from abroad – as his natural heir as head of the international movement. 'When the empire I founded is orphaned,' Freud said, 'no one but Jung must inherit the whole thing.' Freud bestowed upon him a number of honourable duties – editorship of the *Jahrbuch* in 1908, a place on the trip to the USA in 1909 and the presidency of the International Psychoanalytical Association in 1910.

Yet the kernel of a problem was there from the start. Jung always had some doubts about Freud's sexual theories. He was not sure they were as fundamentally important to psychological development as Freud insisted. Freud for his part chose to ignore, or at least underplay, any sign of dissent from Jung, so intent was he in grooming him as his successor. However, an exchange in 1910 was identified years later by Jung as the beginning of the end. Freud took him aside and said, 'My dear Jung, promise me never to abandon sexual theory. That is the most essential thing of all. You see, we must make a dogma of it, an unshakable bulwark ... against the black tide of mud ... of occultism.' Jung was taken aback. 'Dogma' was, as far as he was concerned, an indisputable confession of faith that permitted no discussion or opposition. 'But that no longer has anything to do with scientific judgement,' Jung recalled years later, 'only with a personal power drive.'

By 1912, even Freud could not ignore that his protégé's ideas were significantly diverging from his own. Notably, on the trip to America, Jung cast doubt on the theory that all neuroses are rooted in childhood sexuality. Freud believed Jung was playing out resistance to his own unconscious and was displaying the Oedipal wish to kill 'the father'. Jung, meanwhile, was perturbed by Freud's conduct in regard to Adler and Stekel. He also feared the cult of personality growing up around the movement's leader, telling Freud in 1912, 'Your technique of treating your pupils like patients is a blunder. In that way you can produce either slavish sons or impudent puppies ... I am objective enough to see through your little trick.' Although Jung and Freud briefly reconciled, their bond was fatally compromised.

The final split was confirmed, as Freud knew it would be, by the publication in 1913 of the highly speculative *Totem and Taboo: Resemblances Between the Mental Lives of Savages and Neurotics*. Here, Freud sought to take the knowledge and experience he had gained from his psychoanalytic practice and apply it to such disparate fields as religion and anthropology – a tactic that rendered Jung profoundly uneasy. He argued, for instance, that Australian aboriginal groups used totems as a way of countering any tendency towards incest (marriage being forbidden between those born under the same totem). He then looked at how totems and ritualistic practices served to disguise the emotional ambivalence that one individual may feel towards another (for instance, contemporaneous reverence and contempt for a ruler), in a manner akin to a neurotic.

He made a particularly contentious argument as to the origins of totemism, plundering a disputed Darwinist theory that primitive societies were arranged such that a singular 'alpha male' was surrounded by a harem of fertile females. Those offspring rejected by the alpha male, Freud suggested, plotted to kill their father (the recipient of both their admiration and fear). Overcome with guilt, they then revere him in the form of the totem, in what Freud painted as an ancient playing out of the Oedipus complex.

This was predictably all too much for Jung, who resigned his various offices in 1914. He subsequently established his own movement – the school of analytical psychology that emphasizes the individual psyche and its quest for wholeness. Jung's approach naturally shared overlaps with Freudian thought but nonetheless rejected key tenets, most notably the dogma of sexual theory.

In terms of furthering our understanding of the human mind, Freud and Jung were the two giants of their age. While their split was painful to them as individuals, it may be regarded as a blessing for the wider world, which benefited from their respective, distinctive approaches.

Life is a Balance: Pleasures and Pastimes

'Psychology is really a cross to bear. Bowling
or hunting for mushrooms is, in any event,
a much healthier pastime.'

SIGMUND FREUD TO WILHELM FLIESS, 1895

Freud was a man of work such that those few pastimes that he did enjoy had to be fitted into a hectic schedule that changed little over the course of his adult life. He tended to rise at 7 a.m. and received his first patient about an hour later. He would then conduct analyses until midday, when he would break to have lunch with his family. He next took a walk around the local neighbourhood (usually via the tobacconist) before returning to his consulting room to see further patients until 7 p.m. Between seven and nine he dined and took a further walk, or else played cards or visited a café and read the newspapers. He then withdrew to his study to deal with correspondence or work on his papers and lecture notes, until going to bed at some point past midnight.

Undoubtedly his single favourite pastime was smoking – something he was able to do whether at work or leisure. For much of his life he was a cigar chain-smoker, beginning as soon as he awoke and continuing until he retired to bed. He commonly got through twenty cigars a day, once archly noting to Fliess, 'Two cigars a day – thereby one recognizes the non-smoker.' On the occasion of his seventeen-year-old nephew refusing a cigar, he commented, 'My boy, smoking is one of the greatest and cheapest enjoyments in life, and if you decide in advance not to smoke, I can only feel sorry for you.'

The Swiss psychoanalyst Raymond de Saussure described meeting Freud in a professional capacity:

> One was won over by the atmosphere of his office, a rather dark room, which opened on to a courtyard. Light came not from the windows but from the brilliance of that lucid, discerning mind. Contact was established only by means of his voice and the odour of the cigars he ceaselessly smoked.

Hanns Sachs, meanwhile, recalled that Freud 'was so fond of smoking that he was somewhat irritated when men around him did not smoke. Consequently nearly all of those who formed the inner circle became more or less passionate cigar-smokers.'

Such was his love of tobacco that he could not shift the habit even as it threatened his health. In his thirties he showed signs of cardiac illness and Fliess persuaded him to give up for a while, but he soon resumed. Freud wrote to him: 'I have not smoked for seven weeks since the day of your injunction. At first I felt, as expected,

---

ACQUIRED TASTES

In terms of what he smoked, Freud was constrained by the Austrian government's monopoly of the tobacco business. His regular smoke was a *trabucco* – a small, mild cigar at the upper end of Austrian production. However, he preferred harder-to-acquire foreign brands, especially Don Pedros and Reina Cubanas, and also Dutch Liliputanos. If he could not get supplies on his travels, he would call upon his international network of contacts to keep him stocked up.

---

outrageously bad. Cardiac symptoms accompanied by mild depression, as well as the horrible misery of abstinence. These wore off but left me completely incapable of working, a beaten man. After seven weeks, I began smoking again ... Since the first few cigars, I was able to work and was the master of my mood; before that life was unbearable.' Even as smoking–related cancer overtook him, he would not renege.

Perhaps the only other hobby that approached his love of cigars was the collecting of art and antiquities. As we know, Freud was an enthusiastic reader but his attitudes to other art forms were mixed. In 1914 he wrote:

I am no connoisseur in art, but simply a layman ... Nevertheless, works of art do exercise a powerful effect on me, especially those of literature and sculpture, less often of painting … I spend a long time before them trying to apprehend them in my own way, i.e. to explain to myself what their effect is due to. Wherever I cannot do this, as for instance with music, I am almost incapable of obtaining any pleasure. Some rationalistic, or perhaps analytic, turn of mind in me rebels against being moved by a thing without knowing why I am thus affected and what it is that affects me.

As the figurehead of psychoanalysis, Freud was particularly associated with the surrealist movement. One of its most prominent exponents, André Breton, had been greatly influenced by Freud's ideas, having encountered his work when treating shell-shocked soldiers as a medic in the First World War. The two men, however, had an uncomfortable meeting at Freud's home in the early 1920s. In a letter to Breton dated 1932, Freud wrote:

And now a confession, which you will have to accept with tolerance! Although I receive so many testimonies of the interest that you and your friends show for my research, I am not able to clarify for myself what surrealism is and what it wants. Perhaps I am not made to understand it, I who am so distant from art.

Only after he encountered Salvador Dalí several years later in London did he at last seem to 'get it', telling Stefan Zweig:

> For until then I was inclined to look upon surrealists, who have apparently chosen me for their patron saint, as absolute (let us say 95 per cent, like alcohol) cranks. The young Spaniard, however, with his candid fanatical eyes and his undeniable technical mastery, has made me reconsider my opinion.

Freud was more drawn to the greats of classical art – figures such as da Vinci and Michelangelo, both of whom he retrospectively psychoanalysed in academic papers (although sadly his analysis of Leonardo was based on a semi-fictional account of his life). But most of all, he adored the cultural production of the ancient world. He collected somewhere in the range of three thousand antiquities, from Greece, Rome, Egypt and the Middle East. He also developed a special interest in the discoveries made by archaeologist Heinrich Schliemann, who claimed to have unearthed the remains of Troy.

After reaching London in 1938, Freud wrote to a friend: 'We arrived proud and rich, under the protection of Athena.' He referred to a bronze statue he owned of Athena, the Greek goddess of wisdom, which had served as a mascot for their emigration. Why Freud so loved to collect is a question that has been given significant consideration over the years. Aside from an academic interest in history and an admiration for the aesthetics of the objects themselves, it has been said that to collect and accumulate is an attempt to exert control over one's world. That may well have been a subconscious aspect of Freud's habit. And, of course, he felt a natural affinity with the archaeologist – the one who delves back through time in search of knowledge and truth. He made a perhaps telling aside about his hobby in *The Psychopathology of Everyday Life*: 'A slip in reading that I perpetrate very often when I am on holiday … is both annoying and ridiculous: I read every shop sign that suggests the word in any way at all as "Antiques". This must be an expression of my interests as a collector.'

And what of his more casual pastimes? When it came to cards, he favoured tarok – a traditional game played with seventy-eight cards (a standard fifty-two-card pack and twenty-six tarot cards used as trumps). He told Fliess in 1900, 'On Saturday evenings I look forward to an orgy of tarok …' But perhaps his most curious hobby was the one referred to in the quotation at the beginning of this section, that of mushroom hunting. He apparently built up a good knowledge across an array of species and his son, Martin, later recalled their expeditions: 'Father would have done some scouting earlier to find a fruitful area; and I think one of the pointers he used was the presence of a gaily coloured toadstool, red with white dots …' Freud had a habit of dramatically throwing his hat over a cornered mushroom, to the delight of his children. They did not perhaps realize the significance of his desire for the red-and-white-spotted fungi, though – they were almost certainly *Amanita muscaria* (also known as the fly agaric or fly amanita), famed for their psychoactive properties.

Freud and Religion

'… I should like to add that I do not think our cures can compete with those of Lourdes. There are many more people who believe in the miracles of the Blessed Virgin than in the existence of the unconscious.'

SIGMUND FREUD, *NEW INTRODUCTORY LECTURES ON PSYCHOANALYSIS*, 1933

Freud's attitudes to religion have been touched on elsewhere in this book, but their complex nature warrant further attention. This is because there were three distinct aspects to his relationship with religion. Firstly, there was his outspoken atheism – he simply did not believe in God. Secondly, despite his own non-belief, he recognized that organized religion was a compelling force in the formulation of individual and collective psyches – both as a force for good and bad. Thirdly, his own identity was informed by his sense of Jewishness, even as he rejected the theological basis of Judaism.

To take the question of his non-belief first, he neatly summed it up in *The Psychopathology of Everyday Life* when he described religion as 'nothing but psychology projected into the external world ... a supernatural reality, which is destined to be changed back once more by science into the psychology of the unconscious'. In other words, religious belief is a construction of our own minds – in 1907 he called it a 'universal obsessional neurosis'. 'Neither in my private life nor in my writings have I ever made a secret of my being an out-and-out unbeliever,' he told Charles Singer in 1938.

He broadly saw religion as a means by which society could regulate itself, serving as a focal point to relieve potential sources of tension. In *Civilization and Its Discontents*, for example, he said, 'Long ago he [man] formed an ideal conception of omnipotence and omniscience, which he embodied in his gods, attributing to them whatever seemed beyond the reach of his desires – or was forbidden him. We may say, then, that these gods were cultural ideals.'

More fundamentally, he believed religions – which bear the 'imprint of the times in which they arose, the ignorant times of the childhood of humanity' – are yet another expression of the Oedipal complex:

> To me the derivation of religious needs from the helplessness of the child and a longing for its father seems irrefutable, especially as this feeling is not only prolonged from the days of childhood, but constantly sustained by a fear of the superior power of fate.

It was a theme he had previously hinted at in his 1910 paper on Leonardo da Vinci, in which he wrote that 'The almighty and just God ... appears to us as grand sublimations of father and mother, or rather as revivals and restorations of the young child's ideas of them.'

The Future of an Illusion, published in 1927, provides further explication of his theories on religion. He portrayed religion as comprised of 'certain dogmas, assertions about facts and conditions of external and internal reality which tells one something that one has not oneself discovered, and which claim that one should give them credence'. They demand faithful observance by three methods:

Firstly because our primal ancestors already believed them; secondly, because we possess proofs which have been handed down to us from antiquity; and thirdly because it is forbidden to raise the question of their authenticity at all.

He went on to characterize religious beliefs as 'fulfilments of the oldest, strongest, and most urgent wishes of mankind'. He wrote:

The gods retain their threefold task: they must exorcise the terrors of nature, they must reconcile men to the cruelty of Fate, particularly as it is shown in death, and they must compensate them for the sufferings and privations which a civilized life in common has imposed on them.

Religious belief, he contended, is a form of illusion: 'Thus we call a belief an illusion when a wish fulfilment is a prominent factor in its motivation, and in doing so we disregard its relations to reality, just as the illusion itself sets no store by verification.' While he acknowledged that religion can play a part in shackling those drives that might otherwise work against civilization and cultural development, he criticized organized religion for imposing stifling moral codes upon the individual and acting against free thought.

HIS TRUE FOE

Freud was particularly critical of the 'fire and brimstone' teachings of the Roman Catholic Church. The excesses of a devout childhood housemaid helped turn him against Christianity at a very early stage, along with his abhorrence of anti-Semitism. Such was his distrust of Catholicism that even as he was being forced out of Vienna by the ascent of the Nazis, he identified the Roman Catholic Church as 'my true enemy'.

But for all his animosity towards religion, he culturally identified as a Jew throughout his life. In 1925, for example, he proclaimed, 'My parents were Jews and I have remained a Jew myself.' A year later he professed he was 'glad that I have no religion' but retained a 'feeling of solidarity with my people'. In 1930 he put it even more strongly: 'In some place in my soul, in a very hidden corner, I am a fanatical Jew.' In his *An Autobiographical Study*, he also acknowledged the influence that childhood religious instruction had wielded over him: 'My deep engrossment in the Bible story (almost as soon as I had learnt the art of reading) had, as I recognized much later, an enduring effect upon the direction of my interest.'

Yet in 1939 he published one of his most contentious theses. *Moses and Monotheism* was a work that many in the Jewish faith found deeply troubling. Using psycho-analytic methods to review historical events, Freud argued that Moses was not Hebrew but had been born into the Ancient Egyptian aristocracy and was probably an adherent of Akhenaten, the pharaoh who broke with Egyptian tradition to espouse monotheism. Freud said that rather than leading the Israelites to safety, he in fact brought out only a small band of his own acolytes, who subsequently rose up and killed him. Overcome with guilt at the murder of the father figure, they later evolved the story of a messiah and yearned for the return of Moses as the champion of the Israelites.

Freud's attitude towards his Jewishness is arguably best summed up in a note he sent to the members of B'nai B'rith (a Jewish association established in the mid-nineteenth century): 'What tied me to Jewry was − I have to admit it − not the faith, not even the national pride, for I was always an unbeliever, having been brought up without religion, but not without respect for the so-called "ethical" demands of human civilization.' His attitude to God, meanwhile, is encapsulated in this declaration of 1915: 'Let me add that I am in no way in awe of the Almighty. If we ever met one another, it is rather I who should reproach Him, than he me.'

Exit on Your Own Terms

'How enviable not to have outlived oneself.'

SIGMUND FREUD TO WILHELM FLIESS ON THE
DEATH OF A FAMED VIENNESE SURGEON, 1894

The last twenty-five years or so of Freud's life were marked by an increasing sense of melancholy, the result of both personal trials and the general climate of social upheaval that was bookended by the two World Wars. He continued to work prodigiously and the energy he maintained even as old age and infirmity caught up with him was remarkable. Yet the impression of pervading weariness is undeniable. Take his comment in *Civilization and Its Discontents* in reference to human progress: 'Finally, what good is a long life to us if it is hard, joyless and so full of suffering that we can only welcome death as a deliverer.'

He had hinted at his dissatisfaction back in 1922, in an address to Arthur Schnitzler: 'Now you too have reached your sixtieth birthday, while I, six years older, am approaching the limit of life and may soon expect to see the end of the fifth act of this rather incomprehensible and not always amusing comedy.' Writing in 'Reflections on War and Death' in 1915, he had said, 'Fundamentally, no one believes in his own death or, which comes to the same thing, in the unconscious; each of us is convinced of his immortality.' Yet as his own death hove into view (especially after his cancer diagnosis in 1923), he seems to have accepted his grim prognosis with stoicism.

In 1929, for instance, Max Schur became his personal physician on the recommendation of Freud's great friend and Schur's patient, Marie Bonaparte (and a notable psychoanalyst in her own right). At their very first meeting, Freud made Schur promise 'that when the time comes, you won't let me suffer unnecessarily'.

By 1938, Freud was eighty-two and in very poor health. Then came the added complication of Germany's annexation of Austria. Freud – a Jew, an intellectual, and a theoretician in areas considered spiritually unedifying by Hitler and his acolytes – found himself in a precarious position. This was evidenced when his home and office were raided and his beloved daughter Anna arrested by the Gestapo. The decision was made to get Freud and a number of his family to safety in London at the first opportunity. The rescue was effected in no small part by Bonaparte and Ernest Jones. It was undoubtedly the right decision – four of his sisters who remained in Austria would eventually perish in the Holocaust.

Nonetheless, the fact was that he found himself exiled in England at a very late stage of life, circumstances having overtaken him. Remarkably, though, he summoned the energy to create a new life for himself – one in which he continued to work and publish and to accept his role as a public figure with great dignity. He was courted by the great and the good in his London home. Among them was the author and futurist H. G. Wells, who campaigned for Freud to be granted immediate British citizenship by an act of parliament. Salvador Dalí was another to take the opportunity to meet one of his heroes in an encounter arranged by Stefan Zweig. Zweig had introduced Dalí as 'the only painter of genius in our epoch' and 'the most faithful and most grateful disciple of your ideas among the artists'. As he travelled from Paris, Dalí is supposed to have experienced a revelation while consuming a plate of snails: 'I had just that instant discovered the morphological secret of Freud! Freud's cranium is a snail! His brain is in the form of a spiral – to be extracted with a needle! Though he spoke no English or German, he recalled that he and Freud 'devoured each other with our eyes' and the encounter was regarded as a success by both men.

The same may not be said of Freud's get-together with Virginia and Leonard Woolf, those icons of the Bloomsbury set. Leonard recalled in his autobiography that it was 'not an easy interview'. 'There was something about him as of a half-extinct volcano,' he wrote, 'something sombre, repressed, reserved.' Nonetheless, 'He gave me the feeling … of great gentleness, but behind that, great strength.'

As the end loomed, Freud had been accepted by his contemporaries as one of the giant figures of twentieth-century intellectualism. It was perhaps fitting that his status as a 'great thinker' should have been validated by these and similar meetings, even as he found himself effectively cast out of the land of his birth. At last accepted into the cultural mainstream, yet forever an outsider.

Max Schur had accompanied Freud to London and moved into the Freuds' home in 1939 as his medical needs escalated. On 21 September that year – three weeks after Germany had invaded Poland and sparked the Second World War – Freud took his doctor to one side. 'My dear Schur,' he said, 'you certainly remember our first talk. You promised me then not to forsake me when my time comes. Now it's nothing but torture and makes no sense anymore.' Schur agreed to give him a series of morphine injections and at 3 a.m. on 23 September, Freud died. His ashes, fittingly, were kept in a Greek urn gifted by Marie Bonaparte.

He had, to some extent, seized control over the nature of his end. Whether or not he considered he had outlived himself, we will never know.

Leave a Legacy

'Oh, life could be very interesting if we only
knew and understood more about it.'

SIGMUND FREUD TO ARNOLD ZWEIG, 1932

It is over three-quarters of a century since Freud died and he remains an extraordinarily divisive figure. Many of his contemporaries never doubted his fundamental importance as a pioneering explorer of the human mind. In 1918, Sándor Ferenczi told him, 'Even if our hopes deceive us and mankind remain the victim of their unconscious to the very end, still we have vouchsafed a glimpse behind the scenes …' Twelve years later and Arnold Zweig assured him, 'Psychoanalysis has reversed all values, it has conquered Christianity, disclosed the true Antichrist, and liberated the spirit of resurgent life from the ascetic ideal.' The celebrated mathematician and philosopher Bertrand Russell was another to find enduring value in his work, writing in 'On Orthodoxies' in 1933, 'When I came to read Freud himself, I was amazed to discover how sensible his writings are and how much milder than what passes for Freudianism among the pseudo-intelligent.'

Yet he has undeniably been at the sharp end of a prolonged backlash. Ludwig Wittgenstein, quoted in

Lectures and Conversations on Aesthetics, Psychology, and Religious Belief (1967), acerbically noted: 'Wisdom is something I would never expect from Freud. Cleverness, certainly; but not wisdom.' Then there are those who dismiss him as a scientific phoney. As Jonathan Lear of the University of Chicago commented in 1995: 'Many reputable scholars now believe (and I agree) that Freud botched some of his most important cases. Certainly, a number of his hypotheses are false; his analytic technique can seem flat-footed and intrusive; and in his speculations he was a bit of a cowboy ...'

Some go as far as to suggest that his ideas, lacking scientific validity, have wreaked havoc on thousands of lives when misapplied to people suffering psychological disturbances. As early as 1914, one unnamed American critic said, 'Psychoanalysis is a conscious and more often a subconscious or unconscious debauching of the patient ... Psychoanalysis ... is a menace to the community.' There are many, a century later, who would agree he had a point. But this is to do Freud an injustice. Yes, many of his conclusions were undoubtedly flawed – modern neuroscience attests to that. But no one doubts that the unconscious, sexual drives, dreams and the like all play vital roles in the development of the psyche. Freud gave them legitimacy and made it possible to explore them in a more scientific way. He provided the first, crucial steps along the road.

And even though our behaviour may not be predicated

on the interaction of our ego, id and superego – just as our dreams may not reveal all the secrets of our inner lives – the ideas that Freud unleashed have soaked into the fabric of our everyday lives. They are there in our language, our art and culture and, ultimately, stored away in our minds. When someone misspeaks, or some great phallus of a building is erected, or when a young woman walks into a bar on the arm of a man old enough to be her father, there is a good chance that Freud's name will quickly be summoned up.

It is, then, in culture and philosophy rather than science, that Freud made his most lasting contributions. Mark Edmundson, a professor of English at the University of Virginia and the author of *The Death of Sigmund Freud*, put it like this: 'Freud to me is a writer comparable to Montaigne and Samuel Johnson and Schopenhauer and Nietzsche, writers who take on the really big questions of love, justice, good government and death.' Jonathan Lear, meanwhile, wrote in a 1995 edition of *New Republic*:

… at his best, Freud is a deep explorer of the human condition, working in a tradition which goes back to Sophocles and which extends through Plato, Saint Augustine and Shakespeare to Proust and Nietzsche. What holds this tradition together is its insistence that there are significant meanings for human well-being which are obscured from immediate awareness … Freud began a process of dealing with unconscious meaning, and it is important not to get stuck on him, like some rigid symptom, either to idolize or to denigrate him.

But let us leave the last word to Freud, who customarily responded to his critics thus: 'They may abuse my doctrines by day, but I am sure they dream of them by night.'

Selected
Bibliography

Freud published a vast array of books and essays during his career, which are now available in many editions. Here is a select list of some of his most important works, with their initial year of publication.

Studies on Hysteria (1895; with Josef Breuer)

The Interpretation of Dreams (1899; with publishing date of 1900)

On Dreams (1901)

The Psychopathology of Everyday Life (1901)

Jokes and Their Relation to the Unconscious (1905)

Three Essays on the Theory of Sexuality (1905)

Fragment of an Analysis of a Case of Hysteria (1905; the Dora case)

Selected Bibliography

'Civilized' Sexual Morality and Modern Nervous Illness (1908)

Analysis of a Phobia in a Five-Year-Old Boy (1909)

Notes Upon a Case of Obsessional Neurosis (1909)

Totem and Taboo (1913)

On Narcissism: An Introduction (1914)

On the History of the Psychoanalytic Movement (1914)

Reflections on War and Death (1915)

Introductory Lectures on Psychoanalysis (1917)

Mourning and Melancholia (1917)

Beyond the Pleasure Principle (1920)

The Ego and the Id (1923)

An Autobiographical Study (1925)

The Future of an Illusion (1927)

Civilization and Its Discontents (1930)

Why War? (1933)

Moses and Monotheism (1939)

An Outline of Psychoanalysis (1940)

Among the myriad books about Freud, his life and work, the following titles provide good introductions.

Edmundson, Mark, *The Death of Sigmund Freud: Fascism, Psychoanalysis and the Rise of Fundamentalism*, Bloomsbury (2007)

Gay, Peter, *Freud: A Life for Our Time*, J. M. Dent & Sons Ltd (1988)

Jones, Ernest, *The Life and Work of Sigmund Freud*, Basic Books (1953)

Kramer, Peter D., *Freud: Inventor of the Modern Mind*, HarperCollins (2006)

Phillips, Adam, *Becoming Freud: The Making of a Psychoanalyst*, Yale University Press (2014)

Stafford-Clarke, David, *What Freud Really Said*, Penguin (1965)

Steadman, Ralph, *Sigmund Freud*, Paddington Press (1979)